TREASURES
IN DARKNESS

TREASURES IN DARKNESS

A GRIEVING MOTHER SHARES HER HEART

SHARON W. BETTERS

P&R PUBLISHING
P.O. BOX 817 • PHILLIPSBURG • NEW JERSEY 08865-0817

Scripture quotations are from the HOLY BIBLE, NEW INTERNATIONAL VERSION®. NIV®. Copyright © 1973, 1978, 1984 by International Bible Society. Used by permission of Zondervan Publishing House. All rights reserved.

"Shine, Jesus Shine" by Graham Kendrick. © 1987 Make Way Music (admin. by Music Services in the western hemisphere). All rights reserved. Used by permission.

"Great Is Thy Faithfulness" words by Thomas Obadiah Chisholm. © 1923, renewal 1951, Hope Publishing Company, Carol Stream, Illinois 60188. All rights reserved. Used by permission.

Page design and typesetting by Dawn Premako

Printed in the United States of America

Library of Congress Cataloging-in-Publication Data

Betters, Sharon W., 1948–
  Treasures in darkness : a grieving mother shares her heart / Sharon W. Betters.
    p. cm.
  Includes bibliographical references.
  ISBN 0-87552-798-1 (pbk.)
    1. Children—Death—Religious aspects—Christianity. 2. Bereavement—
Religious aspects—Christianity. 3. Grief—Religious aspects—Christianity. 4.
Mothers—Religious life. 5. Betters, Sharon W., 1948– I. Title.

BV4907.B43 2005
248.8'66—dc22

                                                                    2005047402

For our grandchildren—
Cori Lee
Mark Nathan
Danielle Nicole
Katherine Eileen
Mollie Elizabeth
Benjamin Charles
Emma Grace
Nathan Gregory
Abigail Lynn
Caleb Mark
And those yet to be

But as for you, continue in what you have learned and have become convinced of, because you know those from whom you learned it, and how from infancy you have known the holy Scriptures, which are able to make you wise for salvation through faith in Christ Jesus. All Scripture is God-breathed and is useful for teaching, rebuking, correcting and training in righteousness, so that the man of God may be thoroughly equipped for every good work. 2 Timothy 3:14–17

CONTENTS

ACKNOWLEDGMENTS

Thank you to—

Chuck, not only my husband but also my best friend and soul mate—when the task seemed impossible, he exhorted me, "Write for your grandchildren."

Our children and their spouses—their lives of faith, joy, and ministry in the context of sorrow encourage me to go and do likewise.

Our grandchildren—some day they will know how much their lives, tears, and laughter energize me to obey God's instructions to live and tell His story to the next generation.

My prayer warriors—they held up my arms when I was weak.

Evelyn Bence, my editor—she worked magic.

The staff of P&R Publishing—they made the vision of this book a reality.

Those who walked this pathway before me and called back, "God is faithful, you can trust Him."

My God and Savior—it's all about Him.

$\mathcal{I}$NTRODUCTION

> I will go before you and will level the mountains; I will break down gates of bronze and cut through bars of iron. I will give you the treasures of darkness, riches stored in secret places, so that you may know that I am the LORD, the God of Israel, who summons you by name. (Isa. 45:2–3)

God is keeping the promise of Isaiah 45:2–3 to me. In this book I share some of those treasures of darkness. It's my prayer that one day they will be your treasures as well.

When death grabbed my youngest child, Mark, and tried to destroy our family, I wondered how my heart kept beating. In my grief I felt estranged from God. For more than twenty-five years I had taught women to believe that God will make beauty out of ashes, that he is the Repairer of broken walls, that they could trust him. But on July 6, 1993, I concluded that I had lied. How could God ever bring beauty from the ashes of the sudden deaths of our sixteen-year-old son and his friend Kelly? How would I ever trust my heavenly Father again?

Because of my rich spiritual heritage and role as a pastor's wife and Bible study teacher, it's possible that people who knew me well imagined that my response to deep sorrow would be great faith. Instead, my long journey into the abyss of grief frightened our closest friends and extended family. I raged against God, demanding that he give me back my child, demanding that he show himself to me in the way I wanted. At other times, I sobbed quietly, exhausted from the constant presence of the ghost of grief, surrendering to God's silence, longing for what had been, concluding that never again on this earth would I know joy or happiness.

Early in my journey, I often envied those who experienced similar loss but seemed to be in a cocoon of peace and strength. Though their grief was as deep as mine, they never seemed to question God's presence or love. It seemed that I, indeed, was in a cocoon, but one characterized by darkness that blinded me to God's presence.

Why didn't God grant me peace and strength? Why did I have to struggle to trust him once more? My personal journal is filled with questions like these—and more.

I never expected to open this journal for others to read, but the following account of a woman's grief over the loss of her two-year-old son gave me the courage to write this book and include some of my entries, to help others in their journeys. Jill and Dennis lost their child, Scotty, when their pick-up truck rolled down the slope of their yard and crushed him. In *The Velveteen Woman*, Brenda Waggoner describes a conversation with Jill, the bereaved mother, months after the tragic accident:

> "The books I have read mostly frustrated me," she confided. "Especially right after Scotty's death. Nobody seemed to identify with my anger and loneliness."
>
> "So, it might have helped if someone had put those feelings on paper? The anger and loneliness they experienced as they mourned before they came to resolution of their grief?" I asked hoping to gain understanding.
>
> "Yes, I think it might have helped," Jill explained.

"Although I'm honestly not sure anything could have eased the pain. But that's when I felt most alone, most in need of someone to identify with, to connect with." Jill went on to say that she'd consoled herself by reasoning that the authors had written their books several years after their losses. Once they had regained some energy and strength. Jill admitted that although she'd tried, she had also been unable to vulnerably express her feelings in writing during the time of most intense pain. "I just survived," she said. "I think that's all you can do for a while. You survive."[1]

When I read this, I immediately thought, Oh, I know exactly what you mean about just surviving! But I did record my fresh, gut-wrenching grief. God, is it time to share some of that in a book, to help guide broken people like Jill through this terrifying journey?

I dreaded reviewing my journals for this book, because I expected to see word pictures of an angry, bitter woman, fists raised against God. That picture is there, but there is another one as well. It is of a brokenhearted little girl, begging her Father to explain his actions in her life. And I can see that he is holding me tightly in his lap, refusing to let me go no matter how hard I pull against his grip.

I have concluded that God gave me the gift of wrestling. At first I think I wrestled with him in order to win—to change his mind. But soon the wrestling was for the purpose of resting in him. I learned that he is not afraid of our confusion and needs no one to defend him. But neither is he obligated to answer all of our questions.

A friend of Amy Carmichael, missionary to India, once said, "The woman who has no experiences in the dark has no secrets to share in the light." This statement challenged me with a choice in the aftermath of Mark's death: Would I accept midnight sorrow as an opportunity for God to reveal his secrets of the darkness? Or would I refuse to open my eyes and hands to treasures designed to turn my heart toward him? In time, desperation to understand my heavenly Father and experience his power drove me to place my hope in what I know about him, not in what I do not know. That's when I began to more clearly experience the treasures in the darkness and riches stored in secret places.

Learning to see when the lights went out took me back to the foundations of my faith, where I unpacked each belief and examined it through the grid of God's Word. I needed to know that what I had believed and taught for more than twenty-five years was absolute truth. Through tear-filled eyes, I searched for God's presence everywhere and in every event. No detail was insignificant. It still isn't.

My journal is a written record of the many times God responded to my pleas for relief. It gives me tangible evidences that before I even expressed my sorrow, he had sent treasures to turn my heart toward him. I know now that he prepared many of those gifts before the foundation of this world, with plans to send them to our family at just the right moment.

One other event convinced me that it is time to offer my gift of wrestling to others as a means of comfort. On September 11, 2001, I watched in horror as terrorists rained down grief into the secure lives of thousands. By choosing the World Trade Center as a target, the terrorists dragged families in many countries into the terrifying, lonely land of grief. The Iraqi war broadened the mourning, and the tsunami of 2004 shattered thousands of families. Our generation, like others before us, has realized that bereaved people do not "get on with their lives" easily. I hope this book will find its way into the hands of some of those brokenhearted family members and that God will use this message to help turn their hearts toward him.

At first I thought this book was just for bereaved mothers, but now I know it's for anyone who is learning how to see when the lights go out. More than one professional has concluded that the hardest loss a human endures is that of a child. If God is faithful in that midnight, he will be faithful to his children no matter what they are experiencing. It's my prayer that this book will help fellow wrestlers record their journey through this broken world.

Each chapter identifies a treasure in darkness—a word or phrase that names a bountiful gift that I received or benefited from in my grief. I trust that one or more of these treasures will help you as you walk the pathway of grief. Chapters also include a midnight principle that identifies a truth—practical and/or theological—that I learned to appreciate and appropriate on my journey. This principle is an expanded version of the treasure. Chapters end with a treasure of hope that is helping me more than survive this trauma. This section gives practical ideas for you to try. Here I include Scriptures for your personal reflection. Meditate on these Scriptures as you are able. You may also come back to them later in your journey.

Rather than being simply my story, my personal grief journey is a platform for teaching practical application of sound theology in the midst of great sorrow.

No one responds to life's circumstances in a vacuum of life experiences. Just as life didn't end when we lost Mark, it didn't start when God gave us our youngest child. So before I tell you about the darkness, let me give you a glimpse of my life before that tragic day.

1

$\mathscr{B}$EFORE $\mathscr{D}$ARK

THE TREASURE OF SCRIPTURE KNOWLEDGE

 **MIDNIGHT PRINCIPLE:** God's Word is a light to my path. God builds a reservoir of spiritual nutrients into my soul as I hear, read, and learn his Word.

JOURNAL INSIGHT

November 20, 1992. Father, what is your grace? Teach me, Lord, change my way of thinking and living because of what you teach me.

Ephesians 1: Here I see that your grace is glorious and freely given. I have redemption through the blood of your sweet Son, Jesus. You lavish your love on me. I am forgiven! You have given me every spiritual blessing. You chose me before the foundation of the world to be holy and blameless in your sight!

You adopted me as your daughter! You give me the privilege and hope of knowing you are in control, even when life seems to spin out of control. What courage I have when I know that one day, no matter how bad things are, I _know_ that you will bring _all_ things under your authority. You chose me to glorify you. You marked me and sealed me with your Holy Spirit. O Father, the riches of grace cannot be compared to anything!

Lord, as I read these verses my heart is warmed. It's nothing I haven't heard before, but I think it's beginning to sink in for the first time. Not by my desire or works, but by your mercy. Lord, without your mercy I am utterly lost—without hope. Without you choosing me, I would be lost for eternity. I do not see that choosing as my right. I think I have taken for granted your salvation. As I consider what you have done, I begin to wonder how I could desire anything but to serve you and love you. My motives for serving are always in question in my heart. Do I really serve you because of your great love for me and as acknowledgment of that love? I don't think so. Please, Lord, show me how to discern my motives—to discard self, people pleasing, fear of punishment if I do wrong. I want to serve because of your grace, your love, your mercy, gratefully and fully—completely. I need a fresh anointing of your power. My denseness is so frustrating—so hard to break through. Soften and sharpen my comprehension and thinking ability. Make me raw with understanding of your mercy. Without it I would not even desire you. Forgive me for my hard-heartedness. Lord, I depend on your Holy Spirit to pray for me now, for I don't know how to express myself except to say I am sensing perhaps for the first time my lostness without you. My total depravity. My total and complete dependency on your mercy. Yet Lord, I do not fear you with terror but am overwhelmed by a deep, welling-up gratitude. I can't see this page because of my tears. Your mercy, so deep, so wide. Your love, oh, the power of it. Your redemption, your deposit of the Holy Spirit guaranteeing our salvation.

Psalm 63:7: "Because you are my help, I will sing in the shadow of your wings."

Lord, I'm in my kitchen, but I'm really in your sanctuary. I don't want to leave this place.

WELL AWARE IN DELAWARE

When I think of the home my parents provided for me—and my two brothers and four younger sisters—two foundational influences come to mind: From my parents I learned the importance of family and of God and his Word.

Family Ties

My mother was the oldest of seven siblings, and our house became the central meeting place for family celebrations and holidays that drew together four generations—great-grandparents down to me, a youngster playing with dolls in the winter and catching turtles in the summer (to enter into the annual vacation Bible school turtle race competition).

Keeping her large family connected was important to my mother, but she also reached out to others, as a scout leader and, when I was older, hosting slumber parties for church girls, enfolding the "irregular child," becoming a confidante for rebellious teens. Our home was not fancy, but it was a safe place. It seems the more children you have, the less you notice extra ones in the house.

My mother's love for babies was not lost on me. My life was filled with women who loved being mothers, and I looked forward to having my own children one day. Even at age twelve I regularly worked in our church nursery. I babysat our pastor's three sons for free so their mother could go to Wednesday night Bible study. My parents didn't have much of a social life, so one year, hoping my folks would attend a church party on Valentine's Day, I offered to give up a youth event and babysit my siblings. My mother's response? "Sharon, these children are my responsibility, not yours. This is my time to be with them."

When my two youngest sisters started school, my mother took a part-time job. She loved the work, but within a few months she quit. "I realize the girls need me at home now even more than they did when they were toddlers. Mothering them is my full-time job," she said. I listened well. Mothering gave her such joy. I hoped to someday follow in her footsteps.

Grounded in the Word

My grandmother was a charter member of a little Orthodox Presbyterian church we attended when I was small. In Sunday school and at home, I learned simple children's songs that sowed ageless biblical truths in my mind: "Jesus Loves Me," "This Little

Light of Mine, and "The B-I-B-L-E." At my mother's insistence we learned the children's catechism. When she drilled us on Bible memory verses, she made us give the reference at the beginning and end of the passage, saying, "The reference is the home of the verse. You need to know where it lives in the Bible."

When we moved from Middletown to Newark, Delaware, my parents settled us in another small Presbyterian church within walking distance of our home. If the doors of the church were open, my parents expected their seven children to be there. And there I learned how to navigate the Scriptures—in competitive Bible drills. The youth leader would call out a Scripture reference, maybe John 3:16. He'd then say, "Charge," meaning, "Open your Bibles. Go." The first person to find the passage jumped up and read it.

Slowly, surely, the Word of God was entering and nurturing my heart.

Spiritual Choices

But when I was eleven I was confronted with the need to know Jesus Christ personally. My parents never discussed family finances in front of us; they believed children should not carry adult-sized problems. Even so, I knew money was tight, so when our church announced that the child who brought the most people to the annual missions conference won a free week at a church camp in Pennsylvania, I eagerly took the challenge. And won!

One evening as we gathered around a crackling campfire, a speaker told us that sin takes over our lives in the same way leprosy devastates a body. I shivered as he warned us that unless the sin was cleaned up, we would burn in hell. I realized I needed more than church programs and Bible drills to give me a relationship to Jesus Christ. I asked Jesus to forgive my sins and come into my life that night.

But throughout my high school years, I wasn't sure he had. What if I'd just been motivated out of fear, using God as a fire escape? Did that nullify my salvation? I felt like a second-rate Christian when I heard testimonies of transformed lives. Pride overshadowed my doubts, so I didn't tell anyone about them. Leading our church youth group, singing in a girls' trio, teaching our high school Bible study, being on a Youth for Christ Scripture-knowledge quiz team for which I memorized whole chapters of the Bible—of course, I was a Christian! *But was I?* an inner voice questioned. Maturing in my faith would come with pain and sinful decisions that only God could redeem.

All through high school I remained active in the church and faithful to its teachings, but shortly after graduation I questioned the Christian lifestyle. I'd grown up with so many restricting rules. I wanted to break free and enjoy life!

That fall I attended a business-secretarial school full time and waitressed part time. I didn't hesitate to sign up for the Sunday hours, though it meant I drifted away from the church and ministry opportunities. But I drew the line when my boss said I had to wait tables on Christmas Day or be fired. On December 21—my last at the restaurant—Chuck Betters and his young brother Ted walked in for dinner.

I recognized Chuck from high school; he'd played basketball and baseball and graduated the year before me. As we talked and laughed, his eyes and warm smile—in addition to the dark, curly hair—prompted me to give him my number. (And he claims he gave me a very big tip.)

The night of our first date, anticipating the evening, I ran up the steps to my third-floor bedroom singing, "Tonight, tonight, I'll see my love tonight." Dramatics aside, I had no intention of falling in love. And neither did he. We just wanted to have fun, and I saw tall, handsome Chuck as my ticket.

I quickly got to know his intriguing, Lebanese family. At their house life was never boring! I loved sitting around their table after a big family meal. They told stories that made me laugh till I cried. Chuck's dad and I would watch TV together. His mother and I talked for hours about everything. They welcomed me like a daughter.

Chuck intended to be a doctor; he seemed to know exactly what he wanted from life and worked hard toward those goals. I often met him at the University of Delaware library or student center where we studied together, sometimes visiting labs in the middle of the night to check on his experiments with fruit flies. Then there were weekend parties, maybe at the beach or after football games.

My family also got to know Chuck. He enjoyed them, and they liked him. On the surface things appeared to be idyllic, but, as my feelings for him intensified, deep inside I knew I was on a treacherous path. And so did my parents. Parenting young adults is difficult; as a parent now myself I better realize how difficult this time had to be for my family. I was twenty years old. They tried to treat me as an adult. But the more I loved Chuck, the more conflicted my relationship to my parents grew, largely because his religious background was so different from mine.

Chuck was committed to his liturgical church, and his family assumed I would embrace their faith if we ever married. They understood that my family was from a different denomination, but they did not know that I had been taught that I should never marry someone who did not share my faith. To me faith was a personal relationship to Jesus Christ as Savior and Lord. To Chuck faith was loving God and working his way toward heaven through good works.

Chuck was a brilliant debater, and our discussions often ended with me in tears and him angry because I accused him of not being a Christian. He couldn't hear my words, because my life did not reflect what I demanded from him. Because I was acting outside of what I believed to be God's will by dating someone outside of my faith, disconnecting from church life and experimenting with things outside of what I knew was right, I continued privately to doubt my own salvation, while at the same time trying to convince Chuck of his need for a personal relationship to Christ. Disconnect? You bet. Guilty people who do not want to change put up barriers between themselves and people who represent righteousness. And that's what I did with my family. The more guilty I felt, the more estranged we became and the more Chuck's family embraced me.

Before long I loved him so much, I couldn't bear the thought of life without him. But God, known as the Hound of Heaven, would not let me forget my relationship to him. Unbeknownst to me, my mother asked the church women to pray for God to intervene. One of those women, a pastor's wife for whom I had babysat, was a heroine to me. Ruth Auffarth oozed the love of Christ and never treated me as though I was a kid, though I'm sure I acted like one. She invited me to come for dinner—and listened. By then, Chuck and I were regularly fighting. Even so, we couldn't sever our ties.

Through Ruth's exhortation at the end of the evening, God broke down the walls of my stony heart. She minced no words: "You must break up with this young man and leave him in God's hands. He's religious, but he does not understand your love for Jesus. If you marry him, your life will be filled with conflict. Run away!"

She stunned me with these concluding words: "I'm going to stay up all night and pray that you do what is right!" It was a promise, not a threat. I had no choice but to listen. That night I sensed God telling me that I could have Chuck as he was or trust Chuck to him, knowing the man I loved might not be God's plan for me. I knew what my choice had to be. "I can do everything through him [Christ] who gives me strength" (Phil. 4:13) ran through my mind over and over again as I tearfully closed out my bank account and quit my job. My parents helped me move to Indiana, where my brother Ralph lived. I thought I would never see Chuck again. I didn't tell him that I was going, though I did leave him a letter that explained that I loved him but had to break off our relationship because of the differences in our faith. I asked him not to try to find me and told him I was praying for him to understand his need for a personal relationship to Jesus Christ.

Sometimes the loneliest times are the best of times. That's what happened for me in Indiana. Desperate for friendship, I attended Campus Crusade for Christ events, where I saw young people exhibiting an exciting and life-changing faith. One night to a counselor I admitted that though I'd asked Jesus to come into my heart, I wasn't sure I was a Christian—because I didn't *feel* a before-and-after difference. I didn't have a dramatic testimony. She patiently used the picture of a train to explain that the engine pulling the train is faith, the coal car represents the facts of Scripture that fuel faith, and the caboose represents feelings. I suddenly understood that the train could run without the feelings but not without faith and the Word of God. She asked me to read out loud 1 John 5:10–12: "Anyone who believes in the Son of God has this testimony in his heart. Anyone who does not believe God has made him out to be a liar, because he has not believed the testimony God has given about his Son. And this is the testimony: God has given us eternal life, and this life is in his Son. He who has the Son has life; he who does not have the Son of God does not have life."

She continued, "If you genuinely repented of your sin and asked Jesus to forgive you and come in to your heart but you doubt he is there, then you are calling God a liar. You are saying God is not keeping his word. Is that what you want to say?"

I knew God could never lie. At that moment I chose by faith to believe the promise of God to save me and trust him to give me feelings if that was best for me.

While God was changing my heart in Indiana, Chuck struggled in Delaware. Because I had not clearly communicated my faith, his family was stunned and hurt by my actions. They tried to help Chuck forget about me, but God had other plans. Chuck connected with my Aunt Connie, a committed Christian and my confidante. She befriended him and connected him to a pastor who showed Chuck what the Scriptures said about knowing Jesus personally. By this time Chuck and I were communicating again, much to my family's dismay. And I was writing letters to his mother, explaining why I had left and some key Scriptures, substantiating the need for a personal relationship to Christ. I didn't know Chuck was reading those letters; the power of God's Word was working in his heart.

One afternoon, running up the steps of a college dorm to meet some friends, Chuck, suddenly overcome with his need, dropped to his knee and asked God to forgive him. Unlike me, who felt no great emotion, Chuck immediately felt all the pressures of life roll off of his shoulders. His life would never be the same.

Chuck's new Christian witness devastated his family. As for mine, no one but my aunt and I believed Chuck's spiritual commitment was real. Suddenly he couldn't read enough of the Bible and memorized whole chapters. He knew things about the Lord that he couldn't have known unless God had opened his eyes. I understood my parents' concern, but a month later I came back to Delaware.

Chuck's parents told him not to bring me to their house. My parents were polite but distant. I found a job and my own apartment. Chuck and I started attending my aunt's Baptist church and later a Methodist church. We jumped into ministry, forming a singing and preaching group of college and career-age young adults. God quickly showed Chuck that he would never be happy unless he preached. During his senior year in college, he knew God was calling him to pastoral ministry. He applied to seminary rather than to med school.

Our decision to marry was fraught with family tension. But ultimately God blessed our wedding day, in 1969, with the grace of family unity. From that day to this his family has treated me as their daughter, and my family found a son in Chuck.

Wife, Mother, Minister

At the beginning of our life together, Chuck and I chose Matthew 6:33 as our life verse: "Seek first his kingdom and his righteousness, and all these things will be given to you as well." When we moved into our first parsonage, we were so young — twenty-one — we had no idea what challenges or gifts lay ahead of us.

I loved being a pastor's wife, but we were not prepared to lead any church. God used eight years of inner-city ministry as our schoolmaster. We lived on a poverty-level income. Sometimes I would have to choose between putting fifty cents into the offering plate or holding on to it so I could buy bread and bologna for lunch. But God, through his people, supplied our every need. We told no one of our financial situation, and yet. . . . A parishioner gave us a brand new car without knowing that ours was beyond repair. Doctors provided care free of charge. Our bills were dramatically met.

My own pastor's wife had regularly taught women's Bible studies, so I assumed I should do the same! The older women — some old enough to be my great-grandmothers — gladly came and patiently listened as I explained the Scriptures. They loved me in spite of myself — young, inexperienced, unaware of the life lessons that come with gray hair.

Three of our children were born during those eight years: Heidi, Chuck, and Daniel. My mother's dreams and passions became my own. I loved being a mother. Once a week each child could choose a bedtime activity to do with me, just the two of us. Heidi often chose tea parties. Chuck usually wanted to build with blocks. And they always wanted a bedtime Bible story. I loved reaching out in ministry. From the start we included the children as much as possible in our church life. Our young kids often found their way into the laps of our parishioners as we led Bible studies and other meetings in our home.

In our second urban church, in Philadelphia, young, athletic Chuck really connected with the kids on the streets, and our home became a safe haven for hundreds of teenagers. Once again, I taught women's Bible studies and tried to be there to meet the congregation's every need. The more people told me how wonderful I was, the more involved I became, until depression and weariness took its toll.

Instead of relishing my Bible-study preparation time or opportunities for hospitality, I dreaded each day's responsibilities. I hated hearing the phone ring and counseling requests. With my mouth I pretended to care, but in my heart I wished people would leave us alone. When my doctor warned me that I needed to get away from all responsibilities, Chuck arranged time away; we reorganized my church involvement. What had gone wrong? I hadn't understood that pleasing people is a dangerous motivation for serving God. I needed to get back to seeking satisfaction through the truth of Matthew 6:33: "Seek first his kingdom and all these things shall be added unto you."

We didn't stay long in Philadelphia. Chuck ultimately urged the denomination to send a black pastor to continue the work we had begun. Chuck accepted a call to our home church in November 1976.

When we moved back to Delaware, I was—unexpectedly—pregnant. Right after the birth of our third child, Daniel, my doctor told Chuck that another pregnancy would be dangerous for me. So the news of a fourth pregnancy set off warning bells for Chuck, who hovered and fussed over my health. Some people thought the pregnancy was irresponsible. Large families were "out." My safety was at risk. But I didn't care. I loved being pregnant and wanted a large family. I saw this child as an unexpected but already cherished treasure from God. I even hoped I would have twins!

Let the Little Children Come to Me

In May our dear Mark was born. Seven-year-old Heidi, five-year-old Chuck, and eighteen-month-old Daniel giggled with delight when they saw their new little brother for the first time. In light of the feared dangers of another pregnancy, we knew this little baby was a double treasure from God. Even strangers commented about his long eyelashes that framed beautiful, laughing blue eyes. Heidi became his second mother, and the boys loved cuddling their little brother. Daniel was so close to me that friends were afraid he would be jealous of Mark. Instead, from the very beginning, Daniel and Mark were joined at the hip.

Chuck was happily developing his role as pastor in our new church. He often arrived at the office early in the morning, worked until midafternoon, came home to spend time with the children or attend their school activities, then returned to the church for evening meetings or counseling. As happy as I was to have four children, handling them by myself on Sundays and during Wednesday night church programs proved difficult and reminded me of what single mothers must experience.

But dropping out of ministry was not even a question. Where I served, the children accompanied me. That first year I envisioned and help set up a church nursery. A friend and I took four-month-old Mark on a shopping trip to buy the necessary equipment. Observing me all day my friend finally said, "They say that the more you smile at a child, the more the child will smile as he gets older. You are constantly caressing Markie's head and looking into his eyes and smiling at him. He's going to have some smile by the time he grows up!" My friend was a prophetess. Mark's smile, coupled with his long-lashed blue eyes, was his signature.

Appreciating the command of Deuteronomy 6:6, we took every opportunity to impress on the heart of our children the Word of God—spiritual nourishment even as infants and toddlers. Most of the stories we daily read focused on Bible truths. We helped the children memorize simple Scriptures that taught theology in a nutshell, and they even learned those children songs I sang as a girl.

All four children asked Jesus to forgive their sins and come into their hearts when they were four or five years old. Daniel made this decision after a Maundy Thursday service that demonstrated the darkness of the night before the crucifixion. Within minutes Daniel was hysterical and terrified that Markie didn't have Jesus in his heart. Daniel's outburst stunned Markie, who quickly followed Daniel's lead. To this day we laugh that Daniel asked Jesus into Mark's heart for him.

We trusted that these childhood commitments were genuine but also watched carefully for changed hearts. Because of my own fears that my commitment to Christ was not real and that he had not forgiven me of my sins, I wanted to be sure that our children had the freedom to tell us of their own fears, even as we reiterated the need for them to love Jesus.

As the children grew, we fed their spirits with the Word and daily prayed that the Lord would use those nutrients to strengthen their lives—as it had my own and, though later in life, Chuck's also.

THE TREASURE OF SCRIPTURE KNOWLEDGE

All Scripture is God-breathed and is useful for teaching, rebuking, correcting and training in righteousness, so that the man of God may be thoroughly equipped for every good work. (2 Tim. 3:16–17)

Chuck likes to think of Scriptures as being like little sticks of dynamite, waiting to be ignited by the fires of life and then exploded by the Holy Spirit with power and conviction at just the right moment.

I prefer different metaphors: nutrients, yes, but also that Scripture knowledge is a jewel-treasure that lights the pathway, whether we are walking through sunny days or through darkness. In the midst of the thunderclouds of conflict, disease, and stress rumbling overhead, God always invites me back to what he has already taught me through his Word. Even as a young child I learned the Scriptures, and at every crisis point God reminds me of a verse or lesson from a Sunday school class, vacation Bible school, or teen Bible study.

The treasure of a firm scriptural knowledge was the foundation that enabled us to withstand the darkness that would engulf us when we lost Mark. That foundation is taught, as the hymn writer notes, in God's "excellent Word." Every time I sing this hymn, found in an eighteenth-century hymnal, I am struck by the truth of the third and fourth lines, "What more can he say . . . ?"

How firm a foundation, you saints of the Lord,
Is laid for your faith in his excellent Word!
What more can he say than to you he has said,
To you who for refuge to Jesus have fled?

Each verse of this hymn emphasizes a core value of our faith—that God will never forsake his children. The hymn writer, like the writers of Scripture, is honest about the hard places in life. They will come. But when we know Jesus as our Savior, we will never face them alone:

> Fear not, I am with you, O be not dismayed;
> For I am your God, and will still give you aid;
> I'll strengthen you, help you, and cause you to stand,
> Upheld by my righteous omnipotent hand.
>
> When through the deep waters I call you to go,
> The rivers of sorrow shall not overflow;
> For I will be with you your troubles to bless,
> And sanctify to you your deepest distress.
>
> When through fiery trials your pathway shall lie,
> My grace, all-sufficient, shall be your supply;
> The flame shall not hurt you; I only design
> Your dross to consume and your gold to refine.
>
> E'en down to old age all my people shall prove
> My sovereign, eternal, unchangeable love;
> And when hoary hairs shall their temples adorn,
> Like lambs they shall still in my bosom be borne.
>
> The soul that on Jesus has leaned for repose,
> I will not, I will not desert to his foes;
> That soul, though all hell should endeavor to shake,
> I'll never, no never, no never forsake!

At times, after losing Mark, the Scriptures were like black marks on a page. Determining what to read every morning was difficult, and I needed a plan. Because the psalmists often struggled with questions like mine, I began reading a psalm every day. There are only thirty-one chapters in Proverbs, the same number of days in a month. So I read the chapter in Proverbs each day that corresponded with the date of the month. I added the short daily selections from two classic devotional books of 365 readings: *My Utmost for His Highest* by Oswald Chambers and *Streams in the Desert* by Mrs. Charles Cowman.

When the darkest midnight of my life threatened to choke the life out of my soul, God reminded me through scriptural knowledge of the firm foundations of my faith, precious in the light, but even more valued as a treasure in darkness.

TREASURES OF HOPE

Scriptural Gems
Read Psalm 63:7: "Because you are my help, I will sing in the shadow of your wings." Try to sing a song—any song, even if it's angry or wordless—to God.

Read Psalm 119:105: "Your word is a lamp to my feet and a light for my path." How does this Scripture help you in your dark night?

Read 2 Corinthians 12:8–9: "Three times I pleaded with the Lord to take [a thorn] away from me. But he said to me, 'My grace is sufficient for you, for my power is made perfect in weakness.'" Choose to thank God for this promise even if your emotions deny its truth.

Read Ephesians 1:3–7, which is the passage I mentioned in the journal entry at the beginning of the chapter. Mark the phrases that are difficult for you to believe in your circumstances.

Praise be to the God and Father of our Lord Jesus Christ, who has blessed us in the heavenly realms with every spiritual blessing in Christ. For he chose us in him before the creation of the world to be holy and blameless in his sight. In love he predestined us to be adopted as his sons through Jesus Christ, in accordance with his pleasure and will—to the praise of his glorious grace, which he has freely given us in the One he loves. In him [Jesus] we have redemption through his blood, the forgiveness of sins, in accordance with the riches of God's grace that he lavished on us with all wisdom and understanding.

It's possible that this passage might raise questions for you more than it brings comfort. As you think of my story, remember that I had to choose to believe that God loved me and chose me; I then concluded that if that were true, I was on the pathway marked out for me by him. I will address some of your questions throughout this book. In the meantime, tell God how you feel right now and ask him to begin clearing away your confusion and doubts.

Songs in the Night: How Firm a Foundation

Read, and sing if you know it, "How Firm a Foundation," which reminds us that Jesus—the Word—is our refuge and that we know this through the foundation of God's written Word. Note that the hymn itself is based on Scripture: Isaiah 43:1–3.

Other Hopeful Ideas

Ask God to remind you of the foundations of your faith that have carried you through life. If you cannot identify those firm scriptural truths, it's possible that you do not know Jesus as your personal Savior and Lord. Ask God to open your heart to the love and forgiveness of his Son, Jesus, and to begin building that strong foundation of his love and compassion.

Your soul may be so inflamed by fresh grief that you are unable to remember any Scriptures. Or you may be a very new Christian with virtually no Scripture gems stored in your heart or mind. Even so, ask the Holy Spirit to remind you of his love, his presence, and promises—as you open a Bible or devotional book, as you listen to a friend trying to console you, even as you dream, at night.

Chapter 2 discusses the treasure of journaling. But even before you read that chapter, try to write a sentence or two that expresses your heart to God. Try to thank him for one person, place, thing, or action in your life.

It's amazing how God often designed one simple statement out of an entire book, song, or sermon that met me right where I was. In my grief I couldn't remember very much, so those statements became my lifeline to his truth.

As you read the rest of this book, pick out statements that grab your attention and strengthen your heart. Write them in your journal or on a 3 x 5 card to carry with you. Write out on cards Scriptures that remind you to think biblically and put them in strategic places around your home, car, and workplace so that God will put them in front of you at just the right moment.

Prayer: Open Her Heart
Dear Father, I pray for each one who is fresh in her grief and despairing of life. Open her heart to your love and the gift of your Son, Jesus.

2

$\mathscr{T}$HINGS THAT $\mathscr{G}$O $\mathscr{B}$UMP IN THE $\mathscr{D}$ARK

THE TREASURE OF JOURNALING

MIDNIGHT PRINCIPLE: My journal can become a record of my conversations with God—whether he seems close at hand or far away.

JOURNAL INSIGHT

February 8, 1993. Dear Father, so much is happening in our home. I need to let go of everything and trust in you. Then I will have peace. Help me make that choice.

Isaiah 26:3–4: You will keep in perfect peace him whose mind is steadfast, because he trusts in you. Trust in the Lord forever, for the Lord, the Lord, is the Rock eternal.

February 19, 1993. Dear Father, please forgive me for my spirit of pride and self-righteousness. Teach me what it means to be humble, to be a servant, to be gentle with my words, even when I need to be firm and exhortative. Especially help me communicate in a gentle way when others disagree with me. Lord, please. You know how haughty and emotional I can be. I struggle with patience and yell and say hurtful things to the children. I forget the difference between discipline and punishment. I get angry because they mess up my plans, rather than seeing their behavior as an opportunity to teach and prepare them for life. O Lord, parenting is so difficult at times. I want to be a good mother, a godly mother. But my heart is so selfish. I've made so many mistakes, failed so many times. And I know I'm more responsible for my actions because I've been taught well. I know what the Scripture teaches about parenting. Lord, I want to have a servant's heart. Only you can instill that in me. Give me your kindness so that I will extend that kindness in my conversations.

LESSONS IN TRUST

Trusting God with My Husband's Ministry: 1986

"Heidi, Chuck, Daniel, Mark, get out of the water! Get out of the water!" Our kids reacted quickly to my screams and wildly waving arms.

"What, Mom? What's wrong?" they yelled breathlessly as they ran toward me.

Without taking my eyes off the crashing waves, I shouted, "There are sharks in the water. Look!"

"Mom, Mom, those aren't sharks. They're dolphins! They're playing in the water. They won't hurt us," ten-year-old Dan patiently explained.

We had just unpacked our minivan and rushed down to enjoy the last few hours of the hot August day. This was our first vacation in a beach house in North Carolina, and it came on the heels of four years of intense church conflict. Chuck had recently resigned and accepted a call to pastor the Glasgow Reformed Presbyterian Church in Bear, Delaware. We were emotionally and physically exhausted.

I looked out and felt comforted by the unending undulating waves. As sure as the sun would rise tomorrow, this ocean would be here, waves gently lapping the shore or crashing with fury and destruction. How like the rhythms of life. One minute we are walking in peace and calmness, maybe even bored by the daily routines. Suddenly the winds kick up and life is no longer boring but stressful, filled with the unknown. Yet, in time, God promises that the waves will settle once more and peace will come, if not here, then there — in God's eternal kingdom. Until then, new rhythms blend with old. We become accustomed to a new level of normal. How like my life the ocean seemed that day.

Once assured that the fish were harmless, I relaxed in my beach chair and started thinking about the past few years. My eyes glistened when I remembered the night I asked Chuck to leave the full-time ministry, after hearing a report of a particularly horrendous congregational meeting. The lava was too hot. The stress too much. The root of the problem was not the difference of opinions, which is part and parcel of all of life. It was the means by which a minority was trying to resolve the differences. Scripture seemed to have no place in the process. How could this have happened to us? Surely there was a better way to make a living. And other ways to serve God that didn't involve church leadership.

I woke the next morning, exhausted from the night of tears, still hoping God would lead us out of the pastorate. My husband and I were partners in all aspects of our marriage and ministry, and I was secure in knowing that he would not make a decision based only on my emotional and spiritual anguish. He promised we would make such a decision together and soon.

I counted heads on the beach once more and closed my eyes, thinking back to the moment, a few days later when I clearly sensed God assuring me of his presence and plans for us. Alone, in our bedroom, I had pleaded with the Lord for my husband's reputation. My heart raced. I struggled to catch my breath, "O God, protect him, please. Do not let these people succeed in taking away his ability to serve you as a pastor." I turned the pages of Scripture and read Psalm 3:

> O LORD, how many are my foes!
>   How many rise up against me!
> Many are saying of me,
>   "God will not deliver him."
>
> But you are a shield around me, O LORD;
>   you bestow glory on me and lift up my head.
> To the LORD I cry aloud,
>   and he answers me from his holy hill.
>
> I lie down and sleep;
>   I wake again, because the LORD sustains me.
> I will not fear the tens of thousands
>   drawn up against me on every side.

Arise, O LORD!
  Deliver me, O my God!
Strike all my enemies on the jaw;
  break the teeth of the wicked.

From the LORD comes deliverance.
  May your blessing be on your people.

Wait, what was God saying to me through his Word? As the truth of his Scripture sunk in, a sense of his presence came over me; I tried to understand. I wrote in my journal:

Lord, am I making this up? Are you really speaking to me so clearly? I hear you telling me to trust you with my husband. That he is your servant and his reputation is safe with you. You are telling me that you have a plan, and I need to sit back and watch you bring it to pass. Lord, I can believe this only by choosing to do so, because I feel like we have been backed into a corner with no way out. Father, remind me of these words when I am afraid.

But the battle between fear and trust raged on in my heart. The next Sunday I left church before the service began, unable to stop crying. As I walked to the car, I tried to discern why I was out of control. What was I feeling? Confusion, isolation, and a sense of betrayal. Later that day Chuck held me tightly and once more urged me to trust God to be with us and direct us. A few days later Chuck discovered me lying on our bed, again weeping. I sobbed out my fears as he held my hand. When I saw him pick up my Bible and start turning the pages, I rolled my eyes in frustration. I knew what the Bible said. I didn't need that right now.

"Sharon, read this."

"Come on, Chuck. I don't want to."

"Read."

I reluctantly took the Bible and read Matthew 14:22–27:

> Immediately Jesus made the disciples get into the boat and go on ahead of him to the other side, while he dismissed the crowd. After he had dismissed them, he went up on a mountainside by himself to pray. When evening came, he was there alone, but the boat was already a considerable distance from land, buffeted by the waves because the wind was against it.
>
> During the fourth watch of the night Jesus went out to them, walking on the lake. When the disciples saw him walking on the lake, they were terrified. "It's a ghost," they said, and cried out in fear.
>
> But Jesus immediately said to them: "Take courage! It is I. Don't be afraid."

Jesus' words touched the fear in my soul, giving me hope. And yet I still admitted, "Chuck, I don't know how to take courage. I don't think I can go any further."

Without a word, Chuck picked up the phone and called a member of the search committee of a local church plant that was seeking a pastor. Chuck had helped the group find a meeting place at a local high school.

I had felt drawn to the body of believers, but Chuck had refused to even consider the possibility of looking into the pastoral position. He was not interested in starting over, in helping a congregation build buildings and programs.

God had other plans for us. I listened as Chuck put his name in as a candidate. He hung up the phone and said, "Sharon, I promised you a long time ago that I would never put the church ahead of you and the children. The conflict has spilled over into our family, and I don't believe God's purposes are served by subjecting you and the children to any more of this stress. I'm going to resign and trust God to take us where he wants us to go."

Chuck did resign that position. Though we were broken-hearted, we felt free. Then, right before we arrived at our vacation house, the chairman of the church-plant search committee, Glasgow Reformed Presbyterian Church, called. Would Chuck come as pastor? Yes and yes. The fear of the future began to roll away.

Crashing waves brought me back to the present. I counted heads in the water once more, laid my head back in the lounge chair, squeezed my husband's hand, closed my eyes, and said, "OK, Chuck, it's your turn to watch them." Deep contentment rolled over my soul. All the while we were in the middle of a terrible storm, Jesus' call to take courage and trust him was backed up by his power and presence. God was preparing a place for my husband to serve him. A place for our family to finish growing up and for me to find my own niche of service.

I refused to confront the question begging for an answer. Would we be safe in this church?

On the sunny Sunday morning of Labor Day weekend, we nervously got dressed and ready for our first worship service with the small Glasgow congregation. We had not personally invited any outsiders and did not expect a crowd. But that Sunday the chairs were full and people were standing in the back of the school cafeteria. What was God doing? Within months the congregation raised money to pay cash for prime property; soon building plans took shape.

Our family quickly settled into the church life. Fourteen-year-old Chuck, an accomplished musician, played the piano. Fifteen-year-old Heidi, who loved children, supervised the two-year-old Sunday school class and carried heavy nursery responsibilities. Dan and Mark reflected the confidence and security that Chuck and I felt. Our church leadership was strong and insisted that conflicts be resolved biblically. I taught our women's Bible study and challenged participants intentionally to make the church a safe place for broken people. Chuck also made this point from the pulpit. I had no idea how soon I would be that broken person.

Trusting God with My Body, 1987

Less than a year later I was at home hosting a luncheon for our women's leadership team when the phone rang. It was my doctor. "Mrs. Betters, your mammogram . . . you need to see a surgeon right away."

That call led to an appointment, a biopsy, more appointments, and a mastectomy that revealed the beginnings of stage 3 cancer. The day after surgery on a brilliant July morning, I sat on the edge of my hospital bed and looked out the window. "Lord, what does the future hold? Will this disease take me from my family? I've heard that if I'm cancer free for five years, then I have a good chance of beating this. But Lord, Mark is only ten. In five years he'll be fifteen. He'll need me more then than he does now. O Lord, what is your plan?"

Memories of raising our children flashed through my heart: Reading bedtime stories while nursing newborn Markie, eighteen-month-old Daniel snuggled near my heart, little Heidi and Chuck jockeying for the closest seat to Mommy; opening my eyes in the middle of the night to see Markie quietly standing by my side of the bed, wishing me awake because he was scared, whispering, "Mommy, I'm scared," knowing I would lift the covers and invite him to snuggle in beside me, safe in his mother's arms; talking Chuck into getting Mark a puppy for Christmas because of all our children he needed more than a teddy bear to get him through nighttime terrors; the anticipation of Christmas and fun vacations planned just for our children. Who would take care of my children the way only I could?

In that noisy hospital, my spirit quieted, as God brought to my mind a verse I had learned and heard repeatedly as a child:

> Because of the LORD's great love we are not consumed, for his compassions never fail. They are new every morning; great is your faithfulness. I say to myself, "The LORD is my portion; therefore I will wait for him." (Lam. 3:22–24)

Then he led me to Isaiah 45:2–3:

> I will go before you and will level the mountains; I will break down gates of bronze and cut through bars of iron. I will give you the treasures of darkness, riches stored in secret places, so that you may know that I am the LORD, the God of Israel, who summons you by name.

In my physical and emotional distress these Scriptures reminded me of the foundations of my faith. God would give me treasures in the darkness of this scary journey. If his mercy was new every morning, then every day I could depend on him to give me what I needed to get through it.

As I focused my attention on Isaiah 45, I saw that the purpose of the treasures was not necessarily to heal me but to assure me that God is so intimate with me that he calls me to himself by name. God intentionally would give me treasures that would turn my heart toward him. That moment I faced a critical choice. Would I open my hands to receive treasures he designed just for me, or would I clench my fists and refuse anything that did not fit my definition of a worthy treasure?

I wish I could say that I made the decision to open my hands and then kept them open. The journey through cancer was long and painful. Six months of aggressive chemotherapy stole my energy and my personal dignity. I questioned God's purposes more than once. But he never failed to keep his promise to summon me by name and send me treasures designed to turn my heart toward him. The women of our church took over as many of my home responsibilities as they could, so I could continue teaching our women's Bible study even while undergoing chemotherapy. God used the preparation for that lecture series as a means to keep me focused on him. In my journal I wrote:

This study on the Psalms has brought emotional healing and great hope to me in the midst of weakness and fear. God's words have comforted me during sleepless nights with verses. "By day the LORD directs his love, at night his song is with me—a prayer to the God of my life" (Ps. 42:8). As we waited for the news—had the cancer spread?—God comforted me: "Even in darkness, light dawns for the upright . . . he will have no fear of bad news, his heart is steadfast, trusting in the LORD. His heart is secure, he will have no fear; in the end he will look in triumph on his foes" (Ps. 112:4a, 7–8).

Our children knew I was sick but believed I would one day be well again. They were often the vehicles by which God sent me his daily treasures. For a while twelve-year-old Daniel repeatedly kissed me throughout the day. When I asked him why, he responded, "My teacher said everyone needs twelve hugs a day to live a long life, so I'm making sure you get twelve hugs every day." Mark followed Daniel's lead and tried to double my lifeline by adding his hugs and kisses. Cancer taught me to cherish every hug from my little boys. I looked forward to the noisy evenings at home when Chuck would stretch out on the family room floor—time for wrestling with the two little boys. Young Chuck took the yelling and laughing as a signal to leave his piano practicing, to prove he was the strong, big brother; he'd jump on top of the tangled bodies. Heidi and I watched from a distance; I knew these family times were treasures sent by God to remind me of his perfect love.

Cancer also taught me that life must never be taken for granted. If I could get cancer, something terrible could happen to one of my children or my husband. We were determined to enjoy every day. Whenever Chuck suggested a day of fun at the beach or asked me to run errands with him, I didn't hesitate; undone household tasks would be there when I returned. This moment would never come again.

Trusting God with My Ministry: Spring 1993

Six years after my bout with breast cancer, my love for women's ministry led me to accept an invitation to serve on our denomination's women's advisory board. I was drawn by the opportunity to spend time with women who reflected a deep, abiding love for our Savior, Jesus, and yet my journal reflected more complex emotions:

April 1, 1993. Lord, I'm on my way to Atlanta to become a member of the women's advisory subcommittee. One more huge step out of my comfort zone.

Father, I am humbled by what I am about to do. You have opened the doors for this ministry, and I know you say you have equipped me to do your work. But I am so nervous and fearful. Lord, I expect you to lead me and show me the areas where I need to change. Point out pride right away, self-serving, "me-first" pride.

April 1, 1993, evening. What a good day, Lord! These women are so gifted and in love with you! Teach me by their example how to live a disciplined life that is encouraging. Father, they shared some very intimate details of their lives today—failures in their own pasts, painful events caused by others. But their testimony is of your faithfulness, pain redeemed by your love. . . . Now I understand the passion for making the church a safe place. They know what it is to hurt. I want their heart for ministry. . . . O Lord, please, I want to have a character of gold, but I don't want the furnace, not the furnace they have experienced. But, Lord, I trust you to care for me. Give me strength to face each day with an expectant heart, filled with joy and a deeper understanding of what you have done for me.

During that first meeting in Atlanta, I felt strangely unsettled, as if my life was about to dramatically change. I requested a meeting with Susan Hunt, the head of the committee. I wept as I tried to explain my uneasiness, which I thought was connected to this new church-related responsibility. I felt completely inadequate and ill equipped. Besides that, I longed for a deeper intimacy with the Lord; I almost desperately wanted him to open my eyes to his presence in my life.

We both agreed that God was preparing me for a ministry that went beyond the local church. The time demands of this new role would mean that I would have to limit the one-on-one time I enjoyed with our own church women. Susan urged me to see our daughter, Heidi, aged twenty-two, and Melanie, the young woman dating our Chuck, as my primary mentoring responsibilities. This seemed reasonable. And yet I wondered: Why was I so dramatically aware of a coming transition in my life? Wasn't my response a bit overly dramatic? Later I realized God was preparing me, but not for what I thought.

THE TREASURE OF JOURNALING

When I said, "My foot is slipping," your love, O LORD, supported me. When anxiety was great within me, your consolation brought joy to my soul. (Ps. 94:18–19)

My journal is one of the treasures that helps me navigate in this broken world. Here are a few entries I made during that four-day Atlanta meeting and later that spring, just months before Mark's death.

April 3, 1993. Dear Father, everywhere I turn I see and hear about grace. I want to understand your grace, but I'm afraid I must be broken in order to know you that way. I want that depth of love for you, to appreciate what you have done, but, to have that, I must see the depth of my sin. Lord, that is frightening. There are so many thoughts swirling around in me, and I know you are preparing me to hear you. My mind is often so thick and my perception muddied. I desire to be able to grasp the doctrines of grace and know how to apply grace to my life. I want to live out what it means to be your child. To experience your love lavished on me (1 John 3). I need your Spirit to open my eyes. I want to see Jesus, to reach out and touch him, and know that he loves me.

April 26, 1993. Father, you are so good to me, and I am learning more and more of how to appropriate your grace in my life. I feel as though I finally have a grip on what it means to walk in the Spirit! The sufficiency of your grace is complete.

April 29, 1993. O Lord, how I need you. How I need to be reminded of your sovereignty and complete love. How I need to remember your faithfulness, because right now my heart is breaking. Lord, I pray for Ed and Nancy Lasko [the pastor who showed Chuck the gospel Scriptures] as they face the deaths of their two sons and the possible loss of their third child. Lord, you could have saved these boys from this. Why did you let this happen? It seems so pointless. All those years of loving and investing to raise young men to serve you. Losing their second and their youngest child at the same time. O God, are you sufficient for such a terrorizing loss? O Lord, please help Nancy and Ed to grab hold of their faith in ways they have never done before. Maker of heaven and earth, make their faith real.

So much pain and loss. Why?

May 12, 1993. Dear Father, give us wisdom as we raise our children, especially Mark and Dan. Teach us how to teach them to be pure and committed to you. Make their faith their own. Only you can do that. Lord, help me to order my days to keep an even keel and to get everything done. I want to enjoy this special time in the lives of our children. So far, so good!

May 14, 1993. Dear Lord, thank you for your Word—its power and its truth, its ability to cut to the quick, to encourage and uplift! For the hope and joy it gives. For the little book of Galatians and especially Galatians 5:6b: "The only thing that counts is faith expressing itself through love." Teach me how to love your way. Immerse me in your love and grace and wrap me up in your arms in such a fashion as to push me outside of myself toward others. Remind me always of your grace. Use the book of Galatians to give me a deeper understanding of the doctrines of grace and the freedom I have in you.

Free! Free at last!

May 17, 1993. Lord, please, speak to me with your peace, your wisdom, your comfort. Lord, show me what I am holding on to and make me choose to release it.

Lord, you are telling me to shower Mark and Dan with words and physical expressions of love. Help me remember to do so.

Recently after showing some of my journal entries to a friend, she responded, "I'm terrified by the intimacy with God reflected in the journal entries leading up to Mark's death. Is excruciating pain the only pathway to knowing God? I want intimacy with Jesus, but I could never survive what you are experiencing. My prayers for my children are similar to yours. I think I'll stop journaling!"

My friend's words imply that God wounds those who seek him. I responded to her fear by saying, "My seeking after God did not cause Mark's death. Numerous people have similar longings but never lose their children or experience tragedy. You just don't hear about them! Your longing for intimacy with God does not cause pain or loss. God knew before he gave us Mark that our child would return to him on July 6, 1993. My journal is now a treasure of God's fingerprints on my life. Somehow these journal entries help me see God's hand in my circumstances more clearly."

My journal has become a place of honest two-way communication between a brokenhearted daughter (me) and her loving Father (God). Early in my grief journey, I began to look forward to this time of writing, questioning, crying, praying, and then seeing how God would respond to my wails. In *From Fear to Freedom*, Rose Marie Miller explains the value of such truthful dialogue:

> Suppressing pain and doubt serves only to trap you in a vicious circle of spiritual blindness. You can begin to break this circle by opening up to God and sharing your

deepest doubts—often in the presence of another whom you can trust and who is willing to accept you as you struggle.[1]

I urge you to use a journal as a safe place to wrestle through despair and sorrow. If you are fresh in your grief and unaccustomed to writing in a journal, the suggestion to do so may seem overwhelming. Don't push it. But I encourage you to keep reading—and keep talking to God.

TREASURES OF HOPE

Scriptural Gems

When I don't know where else to go for help, I go to Isaiah 45:2–3 and ask God to open my eyes to his treasures—treasures that remind me that my Father is the Lord, the God of Israel, the one who summons me by name. These verses help turn my heart toward him. What do these verses say to you?

> I will go before you and will level the mountains; I will break down gates of bronze and cut through bars of iron. I will give you the treasures of darkness, riches stored in secret places, so that you may know that I am the LORD, the God of Israel, who summons you by name.

In your journal, dialogue with God about the following Scripture. Does it give you comfort or not?

> "For my thoughts are not your thoughts, neither are your ways my ways," declares the LORD. "As the heavens are higher than the earth, so are my ways higher than your ways and my thoughts than your thoughts." (Isa. 55:8–9)

Personalize Psalm 91:1–6 by replacing the pronouns with *me*, *my*, or *I* where appropriate. When you are tempted to question God's love, choose to remember this passage. Write the passage on a 3 x 5 card and place it in front of your kitchen sink.

Songs in the Night: O the Deep, Deep Love of Jesus

Review the words of the following hymn, "O the Deep, Deep Love of Jesus." How do you feel when you read these verses? Write down the phrases that mean the most to you. Write them on a 3 x 5 card and place it in your wallet.

> O the deep, deep love of Jesus! Vast, unmeasured,
>   boundless, free;
> Rolling as a mighty ocean in its fullness over me.
> Underneath me, all around me, is the current of thy love;
> Leading onward, leading homeward, to thy glorious rest
>   above.

> O the deep, deep love of Jesus! Spread his praise from
>   shore to shore;
> How he loveth, ever loveth, changeth never, never-
>   more;
> How he watches o'er his loved ones, died to call them
>   all his own;
> How for them he intercedeth, watcheth o'er them from
>   the throne.

> O the deep, deep love of Jesus! Love of every love the
>   best:
> 'Tis an ocean vast of blessing, 'tis a haven sweet of rest.
> O, the deep, deep love of Jesus! 'Tis a heav'n of heav'ns
>   to me;
> And it lifts me up to glory, for it lifts me up to thee![2]

Other Hopeful Ideas

When I encourage women to start journaling, they often reply that they don't know how to begin. I tell them just to be honest and see their journal as a two-way conversation with God. Others will tire of your repetitive words; your journal never will! It is a safe place to express your heart and then to listen as God responds, sometimes ever so quietly in your heart. Don't worry about spelling or grammar or doing this the right way. This is a personal journey, and you will learn what feels comfortable to you. I wanted to read every book on grief I could find. Chuck did not want to read anything. It made Mark's absence too final and real. Try doing what I suggest, but don't feel guilty if you just cannot.

Over the years my journaling has evolved from writing daily prayer requests and answers in a small notebook to writing out my feelings as prayers to God. Some people prefer to use a computer.

I'm often asked about privacy. One friend has told her sister that if she suddenly dies the sister is to rush to her home and burn every journal! I do not want my journals to cause anyone pain, so if I am struggling with a particular person, I do not use that person's name. And there are times I have torn up what I've written. I find it difficult to write in my journal if someone is in the room; it feels as if he or she is intruding on an intimate conversation. My husband has never read my journals, but I wouldn't mind if he did. That is your call. This is such a personal journey; I recommend that you keep your journals in a private place where curious eyes cannot casually read them.

Each day, write out your thoughts. Then read Scripture. Write out in your own words how you feel today. Be honest. God is not afraid of our feelings. You might try to write out one question you would like God to answer today. God is not afraid of our questions.

As I noted in chapter 1, I suggest you read chapters from Psalms and Proverbs that correspond with the date. Also read a selection from *My Utmost for His Highest* or another short devotional. Ask God to use these passages to help you sort through your feelings. Record how he uses these passages to respond. Remember that Jesus frequently responded to the questions and hurts of mankind with Scripture—the Old Testament. And we now have the New Testament also. The power of Scripture is unchanging. In 2 Timothy 3:15–17, Paul reminds us that God's Word will equip us for his calling.

If the response you desire is not forthcoming, ask God to help you give up the need for an answer to your question, just for today. Silence does not mean you are stifled in your spiritual growth. We plant seeds in dark, damp earth where the sun doesn't shine so that they will grow and bear fruit or flowers. Some seeds grow more quickly than others, but most of them start in the damp silence of the dark earth for healthy fruit bearing.

Prayer: Talking with God

Dear Father, my journal is a record of our intimate conversations that took place in the darkest night of my soul. I pray that each woman reading these words will experience the same kind of strength and courage.

3

MEMORIAL STONES

THE TREASURE OF MEMORIES

 MIDNIGHT PRINCIPLE: Memories in the context of God's purposes are stepping stones to strength. My journal can become a memorial stone that declares the faithfulness of God in this broken world.

JOURNAL INSIGHT

March 1, 1993. O Father, as I review this past year [1992] and look through this journal, I see your fingerprints all over my life! What a year! Lord, what does this year hold for us? You have certainly drawn us tighter into your cords of love as we have faced the unknown, as we have had to release to you circumstances beyond our control. Lord, continue to force me to grow. Oh, how that frightens me, because healthy growth requires pruning. But it also fills me with great expectation of your work in me. Make a difference in me as I pursue you and get to know you. Thank you for your special moments of the past, but, Lord, I hunger for more; fill up those places with all of you.

May 11, 1993. Mark's sixteenth birthday! I don't think Mark can understand how precious he is to me! I love each of our children dearly, but today I think especially of Mark. His smile, his eyes, his inner self, his attempts to be open and honest, his hard-working skills, his "I love you, too, Mom." I love watching him play the drums and seeing the rhythm of his body. I love hearing him laugh, the low murmur of his voice and chuckles when he is with [his friend] Ryan. Lord, please keep him safe and pure. Move him to you and only to you.

June 24, 1993. Dear Lord, I continue to pray for protection for Mark. Father, he is very vulnerable right now. Please, keep him safe and pure. Keep him from temptation he can't handle. Mark is doing all the things he should be doing as a sixteen-year-old boy. Good grades, working, fun times with friends, serving in the church. Father, help us to be sensitive to where he is and for him to know we understand.

MAKING MEMORIES

A Lot to Be Thankful For

Spring and early summer, 1993, brought us any number of events to celebrate as a family. Mark's sixteenth birthday.

Daniel's high-school and Chuck's college graduations. I also planned an engagement party for Heidi, who had said yes she would marry Greg, a sailor she'd been dating long-distance for several years. The rhythms of family life kept us busy and focused on deepening our relationships with our maturing children.

Life was busy. Life was good. But never without its challenges, especially when Mark got his driver's license a month after his birthday. We gave him driving privileges because he was a better driver at sixteen than any of the older children had been. One Saturday night the phone rang, about ten o'clock—the time we expected Mark home. Chuck answered, talked briefly, and then relayed the message to me. "That was Mark. He's OK, but has had a minor accident. The police are at the scene, and I need to go get him and see if the car needs to be towed."

I normally respond to parenting crises with calm, but that night fear took over. I remembered another late-night phone call, from a stranger, informing us that Heidi had been in a car accident. "She asked me to call her father," the woman explained, giving few details except the accident location. We both assumed the best. I stayed home with the younger boys and expected Chuck—with Heidi—to return soon. But the accident was more serious than we expected. When Chuck arrived at the scene, he forced his way through the blockades, around fire engines. An ambulance raced past him, sirens blaring. He could not find Heidi. Finally he grabbed a police officer. "Where's my daughter?" On her way to the hospital. Though her injuries were not life-threatening, they were shocking and terrifying for a father to see.

And tonight. Would this be a repeat of that night? Was Mark really OK?

I rushed to change out of my pajamas when Chuck said, "Sharon, there is no need for you to come. He hit a pole and he's fine, just scared."

"Chuck, please. I want to go. . . . "

He insisted it wasn't necessary. This accident was not a big deal. Chuck walked out the back door, and terror squeezed in. Outwardly I remained calm for our other children. But inwardly I pleaded with God to—what? According to Chuck, Mark was physically OK. The panic I felt was unreasonable. *Quiet Mark—more like his dad than any of the other children. Popular, great athlete, good student. Involved in ministry. Outwardly confident, but I knew he hid his fears and insecurities behind his blue eyes and brilliant smile. Mark. My baby. O God, please, please, whatever you are doing . . . help me surrender to your purposes for my child.*

Later, when Chuck and our sheepish son walked into the kitchen, I hugged Mark and started crying. "I'm so thankful you are OK, Mark. I was so scared." I could not stop my tears. I kept thanking God for protecting our child. My dramatic reaction confused me, and our kids didn't know how to react to my response. Young Chuck tried to comfort and assure me: "Mom, it's OK. Mark's OK."

The next day at our regular Sunday spaghetti dinner, Mark sat next to me. Before we started eating, I touched Mark's shoulder and said, "I know that no one else thinks your accident was a big deal. But, Mark, I am so thankful you are sitting next to me and that we are not in a hospital waiting room, hoping and praying for your survival. This family has a lot to be thankful for."

Chuck looked at me strangely and said, "You know, kids, your mom is right, and we need to listen to her instincts."

That night, still debriefing Mark's minor accident, Chuck tried to get me to talk about my overblown response. I said, "Chuck, something is happening with Mark. I don't understand what it is, but this past week he and I had a conversation in the hallway upstairs. I can't even remember what it was about, but as he walked to his room, the words *we're losing Mark* came into my head. I don't know where they came from, and I tried to discount them. But I feel as though something strange is about to happen."

We talked at length about our youngest child. Chuck suggested I might be having trouble facing the forthcoming empty nest. He reminded me that I cried at every child's milestone, even when they started kindergarten. Was I prematurely anticipating his leaving home? Chuck assured me that Mark was growing into manhood, being more independent. Maybe I was resisting the normal growing-up process. We agreed that the next two years would be our special time with this surprise child. Mark would be our last hurrah as parents of dependent children.

June 29, 1993. Dear Father, so much is running through my head. Mostly the power of prayer, the overwhelming need to pray, and the exhaustion of prayer, as I think about Mark and how you protected him Friday night when he had a minor accident. When Chuck brought him home, I grabbed my child and hugged him and wept. I'm overwhelmed with relief when I think of what could have happened.

I also have a new realization of how fragile life is—how precious. I want to hug Mark and never let go. But I know I can't. I must release him and know that if he had crashed and been killed or crippled or hurt someone else—your grace would be sufficient. My insides cry out: Never, I will not accept that pain. But seeing our friends Jehu and Patty Burton survive, not just survive but experience joy in their hearts, after the dreadful loss of their twelve-year-old son

Kelly, because they chose to trust you—I know your grace is also available to me. I don't want to need it.

Lord, your hand on Mark is so clear to me. I pray so deeply for your Spirit to fill him. Show us the right balance of mercy and justice as we raise this precious child in the few years we have left as he reaches manhood. Lord, you were in the car with him on Friday night. He admitted he was scared. He's not experienced as a driver, Lord, but you were there with him. Lord, your love for him is so evident to me.

As discipline for the accident, for one month Mark was not permitted to drive unless one of us was in the car with him. Surprisingly he submitted to this decision without argument. As we had done many times over the years, raising our children, we planned to extend grace to Mark and lift the restriction early if he continued to demonstrate that he understood that driving responsibly was a privilege. In the meantime we took every opportunity to remind him of ways to drive safely.

July 1, 1993. Lord, Scripture "pray without ceasing" is taking on new meaning in my life. I am surrounded by people I love who have great needs.

Thank you for reminding me through the church choir, singing "Holy of Holies," of the privilege of coming into your presence with these needs. I could barely get through the song, because it so clearly describes the privilege of coming directly *into your presence. Thank you, Father, for breaking down the walls of our sin with the blood of your precious Son, Jesus. Because of his broken body, I can come into your presence without fear of condemnation. And I can leave those special times with you, forgiven and refreshed. Energized for the tasks at hand, trusting you with the people I love.*

Celebrating Family

July 4, 1993, fell on a Sunday. I sat between Mark and Daniel while the elders in our church served communion. Out of the corner of my eye, I noticed Mark taking the bread and the cup, each time bowing his head in prayer. I ruffled his hair and rubbed his neck. He looked at me, grinned, and then bowed his head again.

We never tired of family gatherings, so we invited extended family to join us that day for a barbecue, to celebrate the holiday and also Heidi's birthday. The sun beat down as my father and I grilled the chicken and hot dogs. The teens played volleyball. Younger kids splashed in the pool, until we called everyone into the house, where the grandmothers found air-conditioned refuge. As was our custom, Chuck gathered us together and thanked God for the people who meant so much to us, for Heidi especially, and for his bountiful blessings.

We dug in to the picnic fare and caught up on everyone's news. Chuck characteristically teased his mother and mine also. Ted, his brother, asked him what he thought about the prediction of Christ coming in 1994. Chuck laughed; he wished the man was right but noted that the Bible says only the Father knows when Jesus will return. Ted laughed and said to his mom, "Hey, if the prediction is right, you won't have to die. We'll all go to heaven together!"

Deeply contented, I looked around the room. *Lord, how like you that would be! You've blessed us with so many treasures. What a gift if Jesus did come soon, and we did not have to experience the death of our parents. Thank you, Lord, for your many blessings on our family!*

A few hours later teenaged friends picked up Daniel and Mark to take them to the local fireworks display. Ted invited us to join his family at the fireworks, but Chuck declined. "Thanks, but I think Sharon and I will keep our old family tradition. We're going to lie on a blanket in the yard and look at the fireworks our neighbors shoot into the skies."

We cleaned up and agreed that we'd had a wonderful day, another family gathering that built memories into the hearts of our children. By the pool we reminisced about the past year. What a great time of family celebrations, new beginnings, new chapters opening for each of our children and for us. Chuck talked about how free he felt since coming through a depression. He described a euphoric moment he experienced just a few days before. He had finished cutting the grass and was standing by the back gate. He looked at our home and thought about the "laughter in the walls," as one author puts it. He looked around our large yard and played an imaginary videotape of our kids playing baseball, building their tree house, swimming in the pool. He remembered the many family celebrations, the large church-family gatherings. He remembered the fear he felt when I had cancer. He remembered with great love the way our church cared for us and sighed with appreciation for the peace and prosperity our church was experiencing. He said he thanked God for the many treasures that he had given us even in the valleys. He remembered the dark times and realized that even there, God was with us. Chuck said that for a moment, he felt that God was giving him a glimpse of what heaven is like.

We agreed that the difficulties of the past two years had reminded us of our complete dependence on our God. We wondered what the next few months would bring and concluded that it was probably better we did not know.

Forty-eight hours later we received the phone call that would forever change our lives.

The Treasure of Memories

> I remember the days of long ago; I meditate on all your works and consider what your hands have done. I spread out my hands to you; my soul thirsts for you like a parched land. (Ps. 143:5–6)

For a long time after the death of our son, Mark, family memories, though comforting, deepened my grief; Mark would never again be a vital participant in making more memories. Even now, eleven years later, I weep as I record our family history.

Instead of comfort, sometimes memories are at first the worst part of grief. So how can I call *remembering* a treasure? D. A. Carson says that our confidence in the character of God grows when we recall our past in the context of his faithfulness rather than in the context of events or people. "To recall our past is to promote sadness, very often, or self-pity; to recall the Lord's past prompts confident prayer."[1] It took a long time for me to choose to remember Mark in the context of God's past faithfulness. But even ten days after Mark's death, I understood the concept of remembering God's faithfulness. I wrote in my journal:

God, help me to remember, great is your faithfulness. Your blessings are new every morning (Lam. 3:22–23). Lord, I'm going to hold you to that.

In my journals written before Mark's death, I can see God's graciousness to me; he was preparing me for what lay ahead, slowly unwrapping the fingers tightly wound around Mark's life.

Right after Mark's death, I often said that when he went to heaven, he took my mind with him. I could not think clearly or even remember simple conversations. My journal became a written record of details that otherwise would have been lost. My journal has served to remind me of God's special presence in the routines of life. He had directed my writing. Throughout the journal are notations about Mark and my love for him. When I'm tempted to berate myself for not communicating that love to him, God reminds me of special memories recorded in my own handwriting.

From the beginnings of building his family, God's children established memorial stones that celebrated his faithfulness. Jacob "set up a stone pillar at the place where God had talked with him" (Gen. 35:14). To celebrate a victory against the Philistines, "Samuel took a stone and set it up between Mizpah and Shen. He named it Ebenezer [stone of help], saying, 'Thus far has the Lord helped us' " (1 Sam. 7:12).

After the children of Israel crossed the Jordan River into Canaan (Josh. 4), the Lord told Joshua to set up twelve stones from the riverbed as a memorial to God's faithfulness—not only for the good of Joshua's people, but as a reminder for the next generation and all generations to follow.

> He said to the Israelites, "In the future when your descendants ask their fathers, 'What do these stones mean?' tell them, 'Israel crossed the Jordan on dry ground.' For the LORD your God dried up the Jordan before you until you had crossed over. The LORD your God did to the Jordan just what he had done to the Red Sea when he dried it up before us until we had crossed over." He did this so

that all the peoples of the earth might know that the hand of the LORD is powerful and so that you might always fear the LORD your God." (Josh. 4:21–24)[2]

In my dark days I had to choose to remember the past faithfulness of my unchanging God. It may be difficult for you to know where to begin to remember the works of God, but I encourage you to try.

TREASURES OF HOPE

Scriptural Gems

Memorial stones to God's past faithfulness are a means of healing when we know he does not change. To remember that aspect of God, consider these Scriptures:

"I the LORD do not change." (Mal. 3:6)

"God is not a man, that he should lie, nor a son of man, that he should change his mind. Does he speak and then not act? Does he promise and not fulfill?" (Num. 23:19)

Every good and perfect gift is from above, coming down from the Father of the heavenly lights, who does not change like shifting shadows. (James 1:17)

We can learn from those who have walked in darkness before us. When in great despair, the Scripture writers took great solace in remembering the faithfulness of God:

On my bed I remember you; I think of you through the watches of the night. Because you are my help, I sing in the shadow of your wings. My soul clings to you; your right hand upholds me. (Ps. 63:6–8)

The writer of Psalm 77 cried out to God in great distress. He groaned. His spirit grew faint. He could not sleep. In light of God's past faithfulness, he cannot understand his present circumstances (Ps. 77:4–9). But then by faith he proclaimed:

Then I thought, "To this I will appeal: the years of the right hand of the Most High." I will remember the deeds of the LORD; yes, I will remember your miracles of long ago. I will meditate on all your works and consider all your mighty deeds. (Ps. 77:10–12)

Remembering God's past works settled his soul and gave him hope.

Songs in the Night: Come, Thou Fount

God used hymns I learned as a girl to focus my thoughts on him. The first line of this hymn is a prayer, requesting God to make himself known to us. Subsequent lines describe our response to God grace, which is sometimes so hard to see or name. The first line of the second verse hearkens back to the Ebenezer, the "stone of help," set by Samuel, to commemorate God's faithfulness. The third verse turns again to prayer language, asking God to be faithful to us, even when we are not attentive to him. Look for one or more lines in this song that speak to you at this point in your journey.

Come, thou fount of every blessing, tune my heart to
sing thy grace;
Streams of mercy, never ceasing, call for songs of loudest praise.

Teach me some melodious sonnet, sung by flaming
    tongues above;
Praise the mount! I'm fixed upon it, mount of God's
    unchanging love.

Here I raise my Ebenezer; hither by thy help I'm
    come;[3]
And I hope, by thy good pleasure, safely to arrive at
    home.
Jesus sought me when a stranger, wand'ring from the
    fold of God;
He, to rescue me from danger, interposed his precious
    blood.

O to grace how great a debtor daily I'm constrained to be;
Let that grace now, like a fetter, bind my wand'ring
    heart to thee.
Prone to wander—Lord, I feel it—prone to leave the
    God I love;
Here's my heart, O take and seal it, seal it for thy courts
    above.

Other Hopeful Ideas

In your journal, title a page Memorial Stones. Start listing the works of God. If you have trouble giving God credit for any good work, start with creation (the works of his hands), promises kept, and salvation. Ask God to remind you of specific works in your life, perhaps loved family members or friends, maybe a special vacation, a holiday celebration, a good job that provides for your family, health, the one person who remembered your loss or gave you a hug, a car that runs, or clothing that keeps you warm in the winter. When the darkness of grief suffocates your soul, choose to remember God's past faithfulness.

Although you may find it difficult to do so, start writing down the many good things in your life that you experienced before the death of your loved one. Each one is a treasure from God. This record will help you focus on his goodness.

We take every opportunity to remember Mark in the context of God's faithfulness. I select and plant a special rose bush for his birthday. The name of each one reminds me of God's faithfulness, for example, City of Hope, Angel Face, Peace, Heritage, Sterling Silver, Scentimental, Joseph's Coat, Lasting Peace. We place flowers in our church to the glory of God on the anniversary of his death. What can you do to remember God's faithfulness to you in giving your loved one to you?

Prayer: Help Us Remember

O Lord, help us to remember the works you have done, your miracles, your pronounced judgments.[4] Show us how to extol your work, to choose to sing in this midnight as others before us have done.[5]

4

THE DARKEST MIDNIGHT

THE TREASURE OF BELIEF

MIDNIGHT PRINCIPLE: Midnight challenges me to believe the promises of God.

JOURNAL INSIGHT

July 5, 1993. Dear Father, yesterday Chuck finished up his sermon series on the marks of a healthy church. He said that a healthy church is a mature church. A healthy church is filled with people who, among other things, view life from an eternal perspective, including suffering. He pointed us to 1 Peter 1:7: "These [trials] have come so that your faith—of greater worth than gold, which perishes even though refined by fire—may be proved genuine and may result in praise, glory and honor when Jesus Christ is revealed."

He cited Chuck Colson as an example of a man who has matured through suffering. On the twentieth anniversary of Watergate, a reporter asked Colson, "What was the message of Watergate for you?" This White House "hatchet man" stated that the message for him personally was that of Alexander Solzhenitsyn, who wrote after his deliverance from a Soviet prison camp, "Bless you, prison, bless you for having been in my life!"

Colson said he could look back and say, " 'Bless you, Watergate, for having been in my life.' Why? Because Watergate led to prison, and it was in prison that I learned, as Solzhenitsyn wrote, that the 'object of life is not prosperity as we are made to believe, but the maturing of the soul.' It was in my prison that I saw that the meaning of life is not found in pursuit of gain, but in the service of Jesus Christ."

Lord, stories like this are inspiring, but they always make me wonder how I would respond to such circumstances. I wish I knew how long it took for these faithful people to come to a point of trusting you implicitly. Did they immediately feel your presence? Did they never question? Were they in a bubble of grace, able to bow in complete surrender in the midnight of their lives? Or did they struggle, ask questions, wrestle with you like Jacob? I think I would be more hopeful for myself if I knew they struggled to trust you. Is that ridiculous? Am I not believing that you could miraculously give me grace to trust you so implicitly?

When I had cancer, I wanted to trust you, and I think I did most of the time. But I had moments when I cried out for you to make things better. Times when I did not understand. I wanted to trust you. I wanted to reflect your glory. But I hated what the cancer and its treatment did to my body. I'm better now, so I can see some of the blessings of that frightening time. We have many special family memories because Chuck and I recognized how fragile life was. We intentionally spent more time together and with our children. We didn't want to waste one minute. . . .

But can I really say with my whole heart, "Bless you, cancer; bless you for having been in my life"? I'm just not spiritual enough. How can I view suffering from an eternal perspective? I think it requires surrendering to your wisdom when I don't understand your actions. I think about one of Chuck's favorite hymns, "It Is Well with My Soul." Its writer, Horatio Spafford, chose to trust you in the darkest midnight—the deaths of his four daughters. Every time I sing that hymn I cry, because I'm overwhelmed by this dad's grief *and inspired by his faith. And when I hear stories like that, I know that such strength can only come by a supernatural work from you.*

MIDNIGHT MADNESS

Whimpering, Whispering, Pleading

It was an unusual evening in our household. All of our four young adult children were home. Mark and Dan had an impromptu band practice in our basement while we helped Heidi and Greg write their wedding invitation. After the band practice, young Chuck and Mark started a summer workout routine. In the middle of their session, Ed Marston dropped off his fifteen-year-old daughter, Kelly, to watch television with Mark. In light of Mark's humble response to our discipline, we agreed that he could drive Kelly home. Around 10:15 Chuck joked with Mark and Kelly at the back door, gave Mark the car phone with instructions to use it only in case of an emergency, and once more warned him to be careful as the two teens left.

We went upstairs to get ready for bed but would not sleep until Mark was safely home. We were startled to hear the phone ring about forty-five minutes later.

"Mrs. Betters?" a stranger—female—asked.

"Yes. Who's calling?"

"I'm calling from the Christiana Hospital. . . . Your son, Mark . . . a car accident. You need to come."

"Of course, we'll be right there. . . . Is he OK?"

The nurse hesitated, just an instant. "He's in critical condition. You need to come right away." I didn't ask questions but hung up the phone.

"Chuck, come on, get dressed. Mark's been in a bad accident."

THE TREASURE OF BELIEF

We pulled on the clothes we had just removed and ran downstairs, shouting to rouse Chuck, Heidi, and Daniel from their rooms.

"Sharon, call Nabil," Chuck yelled as he looked for his car keys. As hard as I tried, I couldn't make my fingers work—to dial our physician friend, Nabil Warsal. Chuck made the call himself: "Can you meet us at the hospital?"

We rushed out the door, telling the kids to come in the other car.

Go. Go. Go. Go faster. Blinking emergency lights. Get out of the way. Don't you know our child might be dying? Pass that car. Go. Go. Go—along the same four-lane divided highway we knew Mark had taken. *O God, please, please, please.* The nurse hadn't mentioned Kelly. Surely Mark had already dropped her off. Or not? *God, please, please, let them be all right. Please, please. Whimpering, whispering, pleading.*

Up ahead flashing lights broke through the darkness. "Sharon, look. An accident scene. . . ."

But it's on the other side of the highway. "Maybe Mark was on his way home from Kelly's. But I can't see if it's our car." Chuck barely slowed down—to give me a better view. "I can't tell if it's our car. It's too badly damaged. . . . No one could have survived. . . . Oh, please, please, God . . . oh, no, it's our car, Chuck. Our yellow beach blanket is hanging out of the trunk. O God, please, please."

Chuck grabbed my hand and softly entreated, "Sharon, this isn't good. . . . Try to calm down. . . ."

Suddenly I knew. Chuck, my strength, my rock. The one who fixes everything wrong. The one I go to when the problem is impossible and with a few words he makes it OK again. Something in his tone. His words. *He can't fix this.*

Chuck screeched into the hospital parking lot. Before the car fully stopped, I jumped out, running ahead, through the huge emergency room doors. Suddenly I slowed down, something warning me that I didn't want to hear the news alone. I sensed Chuck behind me and gasped: "Our son, Mark Betters. You called us. Where is he?"

"Come with me."

Screaming, Sobbing, Wailing

Chuck watched for the turn of the nurse's body. He knew that if she turned to the right, she was taking us to see Mark. If she turned to the left, she was taking us to what pastors call the death room, where doctors inform families of fatalities. She went to the left. Chuck pulled me from behind, wrapped his arms around my shoulders, held me, my back to his chest. I heard his quiet, commanding voice, "I'm a pastor. I know the routine. Is our son dead?"

The nurse nodded yes.

"What about Kelly?"

"Yes."

I heard someone screaming, "No, no, no!" It was my own voice. I felt arms holding my collapsing body, turning me toward Chuck's chest. I hit him again and again, yelling, "No, no, no!" The nurse and Chuck pulled me, dragged me, carried me into a small room and tried to sit me on a chair. Chuck's arms were wrapped around me, and my body wouldn't bend to sit. I was smothering, suffocating. Suddenly I pushed him away. "Let me up. Let me up." I could barely get out the words. "Our kids are coming. Our kids are coming. We have to be ready for them. Let me up."

Just then, Daniel and Chuck burst through the doors. Heidi, close behind. Chuck told them Mark was gone. Seventeen-year-old Daniel started wailing, "My brother, my brother, please let him come back, please, God, please, give me back my brother." Twenty-one-year old Chuck, collapsed, jumped up, and ran out of the hospital. Heidi crumpled before our eyes. No one knew where to turn, whom to help.

Wailing, sobbing, screaming, anger, confusion. . . .

Family arrived, two of my sisters and my father. Friends arrived also—enough that we are escorted to a larger room. I knew from their faces they were helpless, confused, terrified. We were the ones who helped in crisis. The pastor and his wife. People depended on us to be the strong ones, the ones who could explain, encourage, comfort, help make sense out of this broken world. Who would help us?

A red-haired nurse wept as she held our wailing Daniel in her arms. He wouldn't stop. He sounded like a wounded animal, crying for relief.

A uniformed paramedic—a friend and Mark's youth-group leader—sat at the table, head in his hands. I assumed he had come to the hospital because of some other emergency and just stopped by our room. No. He was the one who had opened Mark's car door—to discover that he recognized the victim. Though this man tried—he knew there was nothing he could do. He was in such distress, he wanted to quit his job.

Getting through the Night

I asked about Kelly's parents. We had never met them, and I wanted to see them. The nurses tried to discourage me. *Why?* I insisted I needed to see them.

They took me to the Marstons. Kelly's sister, Kim, tried to comfort Kelly's mother and me, as we held hands and wept.

I also wanted to see Mark. Before we did so, a young doctor approached us. "I hate to ask you this question right now, but time is of the essence. Will you donate Mark's organs?"

Chuck and I looked at each other. This was so foreign to us. *How can we do that? How can we be sure he's gone? How can we give permission? We can't make a decision, which means we can't say yes.* We said no, to our eventual regret.

Nabil took us in to see our beautiful Mark. Obviously he had died of internal injuries because he looked as if he were asleep. He had a little smile on his face, a look of contentment, peace. I reached under the sheet and felt his hard, muscular legs. I touched his hand. *How can I let go of these hands? My baby. My treasure. O God, this isn't true.*

Chuck lay across Mark's chest and wept. "O God, my God. Why have you forsaken us? You must heal my family. You must keep your promises to us. You must."

Thoughts flashed through my head: *I know God is sovereign but that does not comfort me tonight. Because he is sovereign, he knew when he put Mark, this surprise treasure, into our arms in May 1977, that on July 6, 1993, he was going to take Mark back. I know that God did not have to let this happen but he did. He didn't have to let this happen.*

Back in the larger waiting room, I stood in the midst of a gathered group but felt alone. Only God and I were there. *God, I know you are going to do something eternal with this horrible death, and I don't like it. You expect us to glorify you through these events. This is too much. You've taken us too far. We can't do this. Haven't we served you well enough in crises? You are going to have to prove you are real. I will not pretend to trust you. I know people will be watching us—the pastor and wife—and you want us to glorify you through this. I know how to put on the face that people expect. But this time, I will not do that. I will not put on the face. I will not pretend. I need to know you are real because you do something supernatural in me. I cannot survive unless you do something that I will know is from you alone.* Chuck gathered us together and told us it was time to go. A nurse walking beside me said, "You've done really well tonight. I'm proud of you."

Her words sounded ridiculous. *"What do you mean?"*

"Usually the children have to take care of the parents when something like this happens. Tonight you were strong; you took care of your children." An observer's view surprised me.

Daniel rode home with us. He lay across the back seat of the car and wailed—as he had now for three hours. Chuck and I didn't know what to say to each other. Suddenly Chuck whispered, "Christmas. How will we get through Christmas?"

Chuck urged Daniel to close his eyes and try to sleep. For a few moments, before we arrived home, the back seat grew quiet.

Waiting for Dawn

It was after 2 a.m. The house soon filled with family and friends. Someone put on a pot of coffee. Patty and Jehu Burton arrived with Daniel's best friend, Shane. I gravitated toward Patty, sensing her capacity to understand me more than anyone else—because she had lost a son, two years ago, to a brain aneurysm. At one point I told Patty, "For the first time I'm glad I had breast cancer."

She looked puzzled. "Why are you saying such a strange thing?"

"Because of the cancer, Chuck and I realized that life is fragile; because of the cancer, we took more time to be with family."

I don't remember everyone at the house that night. Just vignettes. I remember fifteen-year-old Laura Gould, sister of Melanie, Chuck's girlfriend, sitting quietly on the sofa across the room. Then she came over, sat down next to me, and took my hand, never saying a word. Her mother had died not long before. Laura touched me to reassure me that she knew. She knew.

Jimmy Weaver, a best friend of our children, arrived and sat on the floor next to Daniel, asleep on the couch. Jimmy touched his shoulder. Daniel awoke and started wailing again. Even medication did not settle him. Afraid Daniel would burst a blood vessel, Chuck begged him to cry quietly, but Nabil said it was OK to let him wail; it's good for him to express his grief. Daniel finally quieted down only when his dad cradled him like a baby.

Sometime before morning, Chuck got a little sleep. Though I lay down a while, my attempts were futile.

A Dark and Sunny Day

Sometime after sunrise, our friend and neighåbor Chris came to the door. With quiet, tearful confidence, she took charge of the household. For this I was grateful. Michal, Chuck's secretary, organized an impromptu office in the dining room and answered the phone all day.

I stepped outside. The sun was brilliant. Birds sang. Flowers swayed in the slight breeze. People were leaving for work. Everything looked normal. I wanted to scream at them. Nothing was normal. The world should stop. My child was gone.

Mark's friends dropped in. And ours. Every time someone came in, we talked through the accident again. What happened? Why?

We got a phone call from a stranger who said she'd seen the accident; she claimed the newspaper—front-page-story—and the police had the details all wrong. She insisted that another car—a white car filled with men—came off the entrance ramp, pushed Mark over the median strip into the oncoming traffic, and kept on going. She talked to the police and drew a picture of what happened. They checked out her story and could not confirm it. Finding no other witnesses, they concluded that something had startled Mark, and he had lost control of the car. The drought-withered but slippery grass and compacted dirt in the median probably increased the car's speed. Every detail was critical for us to know, as we desperately wanted to understand the last seconds of our son's life.

We sent Chuck's two brothers and Nabil to check out the accident scene. They came back divided on their conclusions. What happened? We needed to know. But God was not telling us.

My father and brother went with Chuck to pick out a coffin. Chuck told me I shouldn't go, and I didn't argue. *How can a father choose a coffin for his youngest child? How can a mother?*

A stranger came to our front door and asked for Mark's dad. Chuck stepped outside and listened to his words. The man didn't want to intrude on our grief, but he was the first one at the accident scene and the first one to Mark's side of the car. He believed he had information that would comfort us. He had known people who had lost family members in an accident; they were haunted by not knowing if their loved ones suffered, alone. He said that when he got to the scene, Mark was lying back in the broken car seat, his hands folded in his lap, a contented smile on his face. Mark's signature smile. "Your son didn't suffer. I'm sure of it."

And then he left. Who was this man? Possibly an angel?

O, God, I miss Mark's smile.

THE TREASURE OF BELIEF

This is what the LORD says—your Redeemer, who formed you in the womb: I am the LORD, who has made all things, who alone stretched out the heavens, who spread out the earth by myself, who foils the signs of false prophets and makes fools of diviners, who overthrows the learning of the wise and turns it into nonsense, who carries out the words of his servants and fulfills the predictions of his messengers, who says of Jerusalem, "It shall be inhabited," of the towns of Judah, "They shall be built," and of their ruins, "I will restore them," who says to the watery deep, "Be dry, and I will dry up your streams," who says of Cyrus, "He is my shepherd and will accomplish all that I please"; he will say of Jerusalem,

"Let it be rebuilt," and of the temple, "Let its foundations be laid." (Isa. 44:24–28)

This Scripture and others indicate that God takes responsibility for the details of our world and our lives. And in the context of his absolute control Isaiah 45:2–3 continues, with God
saying, "I will go before you and will level the mountains; I will
break down gates of bronze and cut through bars of iron. I will
give you the treasures of darkness, riches stored in secret places,
so that you may know that I am the LORD, the God of Israel, who
summons you by name."

Our own lives had proven his promises again and again. We
had repeatedly witnessed his redeeming love as he broke down
the prison gates and cut through the bars of iron imprisoning
people in their grief and sin. But could we trust him now?

The night of Mark's death I did not doubt God's sovereignty—that he was and is in control of every detail of our lives.
But my strong belief in God's sovereignty made me suddenly
realize that when God gave us Mark, God had planned to take
Mark back before he reached manhood. And that did not make
sense to me, his daughter. Why would my loving Father allow
this horrendous event to shatter the life of his daughter? How
could he hurt us this way? We loved him. We served him. None
of this made sense.

In the midnight, in the darkness, my confidence in his sovereign care did not comfort me.

My real question was not "Is God sovereign?" but "Can I
believe his promises?" We had always taught that God is trustworthy. But could I believe that now?

I had taught women for more than twenty-five years that
God is the healer of broken hearts, that he makes beauty out
of ashes. You can trust him with your broken heart, the shattered pieces of your life. But on the night of July 6, 1993, I

concluded that I had lied. The only way God could mend my heart or give me joy was to give me back my son. And I knew he would not do that. Before July 6, trusting God was normal. But nothing would ever be normal again. How could I trust him?

TREASURES OF HOPE

Scriptural Gems

I ultimately concluded that the only unchanging factor in life was God's Word and his character. James 1:17: "Every good and perfect gift is from above, coming down from the Father of the heavenly lights, who does not change like shifting shadows."

Scripture was the medicine that helped me learn how to believe his promises once more.

Before reading these passages, describe how you feel right now. After reading them (and Isa. 44, above) note in your journal what they say about God's sovereignty and God's love for you. If you cannot find comfort in these passages— take even that emotion to God, in your prayer and in your journal.

> My frame was not hidden from you when I was made in the secret place. When I was woven together in the depths of the earth, your eyes saw my unformed body. All the days ordained for me were written in your book before one of them came to be. (Ps. 139:15–16)

> [Jesus said,] "Blessed are those who mourn, for they will be comforted." (Matt. 5:4)

> "I do believe; help me overcome my unbelief!" (Mark 9:24)

Now faith is being sure of what we hope for and certain of what we do not see. (Heb. 11:1)

Grace was given us in Christ Jesus before the beginning of time, but it has now been revealed through the appearing of our Savior, Christ Jesus, who has destroyed death and has brought life and immortality to light through the gospel. . . . I know whom I have believed, and am convinced that he is able to guard what I have entrusted to him for that [future] day. (2 Tim. 1:9–10, 12)

Even though I walk
   through the valley of the shadow of death,
I will fear no evil,
   for you are with me;
your rod and your staff,
   they comfort me. (Ps. 23:4)

Songs in the Night: It Is Well with My Soul

You and I are not the first to walk this valley of the shadow of death. Others walked this pathway before us. Their response to God's sovereign care when he seemed absent strengthens me. Horatio Spafford is one of those fellow travelers.

An attorney, Spafford was a committed Christian who displayed his deep faith by his personal support of Christian leaders, including evangelist D. L. Moody. But neither his wealth nor his faith protected him from multiple, heart-wrenching sorrows. Shortly before he lost his real estate investment in the Chicago fire of 1871, his only son died. Even so, Spafford planned to take his remaining four children and wife by ship to Europe, to participate in evangelistic services. At the last minute Spafford stayed behind to tend to a business emergency. Alas, the ship transporting his family sank, and Spafford received a cable from his wife: "Saved alone."

Spafford quickly set sail to join his wife in Europe. When the ship passed over the place where his daughters had died, Spafford wrote "It Is Well with My Soul" as a sacrifice of praise to his sovereign God.

If you remember—I had journaled about Spafford and this song the day before Mark's accident. That fact itself reminds me of the sovereignty of God and helps me put that sovereignty in the context of God's grace.

> When peace, like a river, attendeth my way,
> When sorrows like sea billows roll;
> Whatever my lot, thou has taught me to say,
> "It is well, it is well with my soul."
>
> [Refrain]
> It is well with my soul;
> It is well, it is well with my soul.
>
> Though Satan should buffet, though trials should
>   come,
> Let this blest assurance control,
> That Christ has regarded my helpless estate,
> And has shed his own blood for my soul.
>
> My sin—O the bliss of this glorious thought!—
> My sin, not in part, but the whole,
> Is nailed to the cross and I bear it no more;
> Praise the Lord, praise the Lord, O my soul!
>
> O Lord, haste the day when the faith shall be sight,
> The clouds be rolled back as a scroll,

The trump shall resound and the Lord shall descend,
"Even so"—it is well with my soul.

Other Hopeful Ideas

Read a selection from the daily devotional of your choice. If you have a copy of *Streams in the Desert,* read the selection for April 23.

Right now, you may be in so much pain that you may find it difficult to believe that God loves you. It is difficult to trust someone you do not know intimately. If you are struggling to trust God, it's important for you to soak your mind and heart in Scriptures that tell you the truth about his love and character. We are more alert to his directions and guidance when the lights are out. The darkness becomes a conduit of his love.

Prayer: Believing Promises

O Father, please enable each of us to believe your promises, especially in the midnights of life.

5

$\mathscr{L}$EANING INTO THE $\mathscr{P}$AIN

THE TREASURE OF TEARS

MIDNIGHT PRINCIPLE: God knows about and treasures every one of my tears.

JOURNAL INSIGHT

July 9, 1993. We decided not to have a public viewing of Mark's body. Just family and Mark's best friends. He looked so peaceful. His mouth curved in his smile, like he had a private joke. All of us noticed it. How trite I sound. Clichéd. My child. My sweet surprise baby. Dead. Lifeless. No. No. No. When we arrived back home, the kids asked us to listen to "The Last Time I Fall," a song they think of as Mark's song. I listened and cried and have hope. Yes. Mark struggled to choose righteousness and he often failed. One particular time when he was caught in his sin, he suddenly cried out, "I'm bad, I'm bad, I'm bad! I can't be good!" Chuck used that moment to lead Mark once more to the cross and to be sure of his personal relationship to Christ. To affirm his childhood commitment to Jesus.

Mark will never say words like that again. He has fallen one last time—not in temptation but in worship of the only One who can make him righteous. What was it like for my child when he saw Jesus? This one whose smile charmed and whose heart made the left out feel included? Mark, the one who cried out his anguish and inability to resist temptation, the son who told his friends he wanted to be a pastor like his dad. He wanted to be a man, respected as a man, not as the youngest child. Oh, Mark, you are complete now. You are in heaven because you are clothed in the righteousness of Christ. You understand grace in a way you never could on earth. You know more than your mom and dad! You are with Jesus, like Jesus.

O God, help me. Keep me from falling into sin as I try to walk by faith in this foreign land of grief. Let my only fall be in worship of the One who made heaven possible for my child.

A GHASTLY GRIEF

Laid to Rest

In the days after Mark's death, God did not robe me in a cocoon of peace and grace. Instead I suffocated in a garb of ghastly grief that I feared would strangle every breath of life out of me. I knew that others had experienced similar loss yet never questioned the presence or promises of God. Their grief was no less than mine, but they seemed to be in a garment of grace. I envied them. I wanted that covering, that indescribable submission to God's purposes, trusting him to do all things well. I begged God to give me that same sensation. I cried out for him to speak to me, to let me feel his presence. But I soon realized I did not know how to trust God and grieve for my son at the same time. Trusting God seemed to say that it was all right that Mark was gone. It wasn't all right. Trusting God seemed to be leaving Mark behind. I could not do that. Despair. Despair. Oh, such despair. Would I ever feel God's love again?

God had used the hymn "O, the Deep, Deep Love of Jesus" to teach me about his love, so I requested it at the beginning of Mark's funeral, which we chose to call a coronation service. As the congregation of more than fifteen hundred stood, Chuck put his arm around me and whispered, "Just sit and listen to me say the words." I wearily closed my eyes, laid my head on Chuck's shoulder, and tried to absorb his familiar strength into my soul. I listened to the song, but all I heard were men's deep voices, singing in a minor key. I envisioned black-cloaked monks, holding candles and processing toward the front of the church. How I needed to believe the words, that the deep, deep love of Jesus would flow over us and sustain us, even in this darkness.

The morning after the coronation service, a limousine picked up our family to take us to the committal service. My childhood pastor, Bob Auffarth, met us at the cemetery and offered to handle the short service for Chuck. Chuck refused and led us to the reserved chairs. Later he told me that as he stood by the casket the reality of what he was doing slammed his heart. He could barely breathe and wished he had accepted Bob's offer. As he quoted the profound proclamation, "O death, where is your victory, O grave, where is your sting?" (1 Cor. 15:55), I rose from my chair and hugged him. He asked our friends and family to sing a short chorus: "Father, we love you, we worship and adore you." Then he grabbed my hand and pulled all of us back to the car and home where friends and family joined us for lunch.

Months later we set a grave marker, engraved with the phrase "With Jesus, Like Jesus" and one of Mark's favorite Scriptures, Psalm 139:15–16: "My frame was not hidden from you when I was made in the secret place. When I was woven together in the depths of the earth, your eyes saw my unformed body. All the days ordained for me were written in your book before one of them came to be."

Though we thoughtfully laid Mark to rest, my spirit was anywhere but at rest.

The First Weeks in Darkness

Laughter and tears filled our house that afternoon. I slipped away to our bedroom to try to sort through some of my questions. My four sisters quietly followed me and sat on the floor as I lay on our bed and tried to verbalize what I was feeling. It was an impossible task.

It was even harder to realize that another family was experiencing equal grief. Kelly's parents had called us that week to share our sorrow and to make sure the services for our children did not overlap. They told us that Kelly had liked Mark since meeting him in sixth grade. Mark had been to their home, and they loved him. Soon our children and their daughter, Kim, found great comfort in spending time together and talking about their brother and sister.

About a week after the accident, Ed, Kelly's dad, called and asked if we knew who had put the crosses on the highway at the accident site. We were stunned but thrilled by this anonymous carpenter. We asked around but no one seemed to know. The crosses reminded us that the accident scene was a holy place, the place where Mark and Kelly saw Jesus. We respected the desire of the giver and stopped trying to learn his identity.

For over a year my sister Jane Anne called every day and encouraged me to cry and talk honestly. Short visits of family and friends broke up the dragging days and evenings. Our children's friends were a special and steady comfort to the whole family.

Because of the prayers of our friends, most nights we fell into bed and slept soundly. And yet I dreaded the nights, because I would have to wake up and face another morning. I went to bed crying, woke up crying. Leaving the house was hard. This puzzled me until I realized that being at home made me feel closer to Mark. Entering the world outside our home confronted me with the reality of his absence.

I never understood what grief experts call the denial stage. How could you deny that someone had died? But to survive terrible loss, it seems that we subconsciously tuck away some of our grief; we can't handle all of it at one time.

One night Chuck called us all together and said, "Let's get these thank-you letters signed." I had wanted to write a personal note to each person, but, having no energy for such a job, we sent the same letter to everyone, hoping people would understand.

Sensing that my daily task was grief work, I read every book I could find on grief, searching for a map through this terrifying terrain. Chuck didn't want to read any books but gladly listened to insights I found and had recorded in my journal.

As a pastor's wife, I had seen enough grief-stricken people wrapped in unhealthy despair, locked in their bitterness, anger, and destructive passion for what was. They were frozen in time, refusing the comfort and strength promised by the Word of God. My lifetime relationship to God through his Son, Jesus, taught me that my only hope for redeeming this horrific pain was through his power and presence. I needed to more than believe this truth. I needed to experience it. I wanted to know that everything I believed and taught about God and his Word was true. Yet to question God seemed blasphemous and terrifying. Was I sinning?

When we are in despair, it's difficult to take even one step forward. My journal is one place where I vigorously fought despair. In these entries you will see that I write what I am thinking and then turn to Scripture or a trusted devotional for God's response. The following are typical journal entries:

July 16. Lord, I'd do anything to get Mark back. Anything. I don't have the words to express my longing for what was. I walk through the house and see him frozen in time. We will never have another picture of him past this age. I cry out to you. How could you wound us this way? I think about Chuck's prayer, "Lord, heal this family. You've wounded us."

July 20. O God, others have walked this pathway of sorrow before me. Please show me in your Word how to walk by faith. I need someone, anyone, who will show me how to reconcile your love with your sovereignty. I don't know how to do this. I am so afraid. I want my child back. Please, God, please, help me. These events do not make me feel loved by you. You lead me to Psalm 73:21–26:

> When my heart was grieved and my spirit embittered, I was senseless and ignorant; I was a brute beast before you. Yet I am always with you; you hold me by my right hand. You guide me with your counsel, and afterward you will take me into glory. Whom have I in heaven but you? And being with you, I desire nothing on earth. My flesh and my heart may fail, but God is the strength of my heart and my portion forever.

The psalmist is honest about his struggle to reconcile his circumstances with his feelings and his expectations of you. He concludes that if he doesn't have you, he has nothing. That when everything else fails, you don't. Lord, I want to believe that but right now I don't.

July 24. This is a bad day, and it's only 7:30 a.m. I can't stop crying. I hurt physically. I miss Mark. I can't do what you are demanding. I can't go on with joy in my life. Joy: perfect acquiescence to the will of God. I can't acquiesce. My chest hurts and my stomach aches. My throat hurts from trying not to cry. Tears are a release, yes wailing also helps. Some say life must move on. But how can it? You lead me to 2 Peter 1:3: "His divine power has given us everything we need for life and godliness through our knowledge of him who called us by his own glory and goodness."

According to this passage, you have placed within me everything I need to be complete in you.

Psalm 139:16: "All the days ordained for me were written in your book before one of them came to be."

All our days are in your book. So, Lord, if my days are ordained by you, then my needs are going to be met by you. When you call me to a task, you equip me for it. If only I could stop crying. I know I have to walk through this pathway of suffering. My healing will not come unless I lean into the pain. This feels like major surgery without an anesthetic. I know now that your grace is not an anesthetic. Then what is your grace? You say that your yoke is easy and your burden light. This yoke is strangling me; it is not light. Lord, please get me through this day. This hour. This moment. Help me to function.

Roberta called and I cried as she read 1 Peter 5:10-11: "And the God of all grace, who called you to his eternal glory in Christ, after you have suffered a little while, will himself restore you and make you strong, firm and steadfast. To him be the power forever and ever. Amen."

You promise to settle me <u>after</u> I have suffered a little while. Your definition of a "little while" scares me. Lord, settle me, settle me.

Joan called and prayed with me. I felt more settled and was able to rest.

July 27. Dear Lord, it's been three weeks since we last saw Mark. Never have we been separated from any of our children for such a long period. . . . Early this morning I heard footsteps in the hallway. In the fog of sleep, I thought it was Mark. Then reality stuck. It was Greg getting ready for work. I felt as though the only way my heavy heart could be lifted was for Mark to step through the door. Is this what the experts call denial? Thinking that you are going to give him back. But, no, you're not giving him back in this lifetime.

Even as I gave in to my soul loneliness, I heard you call me to yourself. I want to talk to someone who will explain this to me. Put together the puzzle parts. And I hear you say, "Sharon, talk to me. Listen to me. I'll gently rub the ointment of my love into your deep wound." I have a new realization of your hatred for death—our enemy—a new understanding of the need for Christ to die and then conquer death—to look it in the face and say "Death, where is your sting? Where is your victory?"

Why didn't I ever grasp the depth of those words before? The same words I've heard so many times and acknowledged my belief in their power. But now, now I deeply hang on to their meaning. Death is swallowed up by the resurrection of Christ. My precious Mark. How I want him here. But how grateful I am that I know without a doubt he is alive. I will not say good-bye to my sweet boy. I will hold on to the hope and absolute guarantee of being with him again.

July 29. Well, Lord, you have not answered my prayer. My heart is not steady, my path is not level. I am experiencing every emotion possible. Wednesday night Chuck, Heidi, and young Chuck talked about heaven and Mark being there. I kept staring at the picture we took of him coming down the steps at his sixteenth birthday party. For a split second, I had such a sense of joy and wonder as I imagined Mark experiencing heaven for the first time. How could that moment slip away so quickly?

I took Dan to work and passed the accident scene for the first time. Lord, I want to think of that place as holy and sacred. You were there to take Mark and Kelly home. Father, please, make me thank you for that every time.

Thursday was horrid. Grocery shopping for the first time. Without thinking, I placed some of Mark's favorite foods in the basket. Then I remembered. Mark is not here.

Everywhere I looked, I saw his favorite foods. So much of my identity is wrapped up in preparing favorite meals for people I love. I cried as I walked down the aisles, not caring who saw me, wanting to scream at people wheeling their children through the store. "Why are you so normal? Don't you understand, my child is gone! Why aren't you crying? Why aren't you hugging your children?" I see a mother yank her child's arm, and I want to yank her. I didn't know I could be so angry, so broken. The stench of death permeates me. I leave my cart of food, rush home, run upstairs, into our bathroom, closing every door behind me, collapse on the floor, stuff a washcloth in my mouth to silence my wails.

You remind me that now I must choose to remember that Mark is at the banquet table brimming with every good food. He doesn't need me anymore. I want my child to need me. I wasn't finished being his mother.

Thursday night I wrapped Mark's robe around me like a big cocoon, trying to breathe in his scent, his warmth, weeping for my child. Curled up in a tight ball on our bed. Desolation, isolation. Despair. Emotionally and spiritually wrestling, wrestling. Longing to run away from my faith, from you. If only I didn't have three other children who are watching me, who might be tempted to copy my faithlessness. I don't want them to walk in bitterness and isolation from you. I know you

are their only hope. . . . For an instance I think I'm willing
to reject you, but I don't want my children to. If I don't
think you are enough for me, why do I want our children to
trust you? I must be crazy. Despair.

Job's Comforters

On Sunday evening, August 1, Chuck and I were home
alone and feeling utterly empty. Chuck reminded me that we
must choose to walk by faith, choose to do what is right and helpful in spite of our emotions. In an attempt to move us away from
our gloom, Chuck suggested we get out of the house, go to a setting where the Word of God would be preeminent. We went to
a local Bible conference. I wrote in my journal the next day:

We settle in to our seats and wait, with renewed hope for you
to miraculously speak to our hearts through your spokesman,
the preacher. His topic: "How to Live a Long Life." His
premise: If we obey God's rules, God is obligated to give us
many years on this earth. Therefore, if someone dies young,
it's because of God's judgment and wrath on that person.

Rage-filled thoughts race through my head: "What
about Jesus? He was young! What about the people God
describes in Hebrews 11 who were tortured and died because of
their faith, not because of their faithlessness? This sounds like
the message of Job's comforters." By the end of the sermon I
want to accost the speaker. "You have shamefully distorted
God's Word!" Chuck urges me to settle down. A friend

comes up to offer his condolences and then hands us a piece of paper with the name and phone number of Marilyn Heavilin, a mother who has lost three sons. Our friend offers her as a source of help and comfort.

On our way home, I tell Chuck I am fearful of losing my mind. We had gone to that service looking for help. Why didn't God comfort us? We arrived home in a worse state than when we had left. I went to bed sobbing. I woke up sobbing.

I am losing hope, losing my mind. I want to start screaming and never stop. . . . Chuck's mother comes by. She looks terrible but wants to be with us, to share in our sorrow. She is in deep grief, and we can't help her. In desperate need for hope, I call the stranger, Marilyn Heavilin.

Permission to Grieve Honestly

It seems God sent us to that Bible conference not so much to hear the sermon as to connect me with a woman whose personal experience belied the preacher's message.

I could barely speak through the sobs and repeatedly apologized for my tears. "Marilyn, I miss Mark in ways I can't describe. This ache refuses to stop. But even more terrifying is that I'm afraid I am losing my mind and my faith. I thought I knew God, but I now realize I don't. Nothing in my life is secure. What if he hurts me again? I have never felt such sorrow and disappointment with my heavenly Father. Am I crazy? Will I ever trust God again? I know he doesn't have to give me any answers. . . . What answer would be good enough? I know he doesn't owe me anything. . . . Will I ever feel good again? How long will this anguish strangle me?"

Marilyn responded, "Sharon, you are not crazy. You are brokenhearted. You are a mother. You miss your child. You are exactly where you should be. God is not afraid of your questions. He needs no one to defend him. He even invites you to come to him with your doubts, your fears, your longings."

Though we had never met, I knew I had found a soul-friend. Here was a credible witness to the faithfulness of God. She had experienced his presence in the darkness of death not once but three times. She understood and did not condemn my wild emotions. I told her that I did not feel God's love. He seemed like a stranger. My new friend encouraged me, "That's OK. Keep being honest with God and seeking him. And one day, as you come to the other side of this sorrow, you will understand his love in a way you never have before."

I hesitated before responding. "Marilyn, I do not even know what his love means. I can't comprehend what you are saying."

Marilyn gently answered, "I know you don't. And that's OK, too. Just believe me. He's not afraid of your questions. He's holding you tightly in his grip and will never let you go."

That phone conversation was a turning point for me. The ache was still there, and I knew the journey would be arduous. But Marilyn gave me permission to grieve honestly as a mother, not a pastor's wife. She assured me I wasn't crazy, just brokenhearted. She refused to put our grief on a timeline. She reminded me that God's children are safely in his grip. She encouraged me to wrestle with God, which is the topic of my

next chapter. Marilyn gave me hope that one day the inflammation of my broken heart would subside just enough for me to feel
God's presence and love once more. For the first time since July
6, I had hope. I began to understand that the darker the despair,
the more brilliant the light of God's love.

THE TREASURE OF TEARS

Oh, that my head were a spring of water
 and my eyes a fountain of tears!
I would weep day and night
 for the slain of my people! (Jer. 9:1)

My newly divorced friend finished a description of her
tumultuous marriage break-up with these words, "I didn't know
I had so many tears. Just when I think I've run out, something
happens and they start all over again. Mostly I'm exhausted from
crying. But sometimes they are cleansing and afterwards, I'm
ready to face the next hard step."

Tears of grief and even despair—the tears themselves are a
treasure in the darkness. I say that on the basis of the psalmist's
prayer: "Put thou my tears into thy bottle: are they not in thy
book?" (Ps. 56:8 KJV).

In an article on the benefit of tears, Cathy McBride notes
that she finds encouragement in seeing "that many of the Bible
characters who developed the strongest faith wept openly.
Joseph, Hannah, Paul, Peter, Mary Magdalene, and the prophets
Ezra and Hezekiah."[1] And Jeremiah is sometimes called the
weeping prophet.

I can completely relate to a heart-wrenching scene recorded
in 2 Samuel 18, when King David hears of the tragic death of his
son. "The king was shaken. He went up to the room over the
gateway and wept. As he went, he said: "My son, my son

Absalom! If only I had died instead of you—O Absalom, my son, my son!" (2 Sam. 18:33).

People experiencing deep loss often can't adequately describe the black abyss of sorrow and despair. And my experience, though similar to yours, is not exactly the same as yours. Your relationship to your loved one or child is unique. Your response to his or her physical absence will reflect that uniqueness. There is no easy remedy for your broken heart. The journey is long and hard.

At first Chuck and I were afraid that if we surrendered to the soul grief, we would never stop crying. Chuck especially fought the assault of tears, because it took several days for him to physically recover. But resisting the tears was also exhausting, so he began to go to the cemetery, turn on loud worship music, and privately wail.

I chose to cry uncontrollably when the house was empty. I wondered if the neighbors could hear me. I warn friends and family of freshly bereaved people not to be frightened of sudden outbursts, often followed by exhaustion or laughter over a sweet memory.

In *Keeper of the Springs*, Ingrid Trobisch eloquently describes the role of tears in the grief journey:

> Edith Schaeffer wrote, "Don't abort your afflictions." In other words, we do well to embrace the pain until its work is done. The human spirit in adversity can be a wondrous thing. Allow tears to flow. Scientists tell us they wash toxic chemicals from our bodies. Psychologists say they wash pain out of our hearts.
>
> Tears are the price we pay for loving. Unless grief-work is done, a person is kept from being fully alive. "Blessed are those who mourn," the Bible says, "for they will be comforted" (Matt. 5:4). Mourning is never easy and lasts longer than most people expect. . . . Crying

buckets of tears is a journey. It takes us from where we were before loss to where we'll be once we've adapted to the changes loss brings. No one can measure when those days are over. It requires patience with ourselves and with those who insinuate we should hurry up and get over it. . . . I believe patience is the continuous process of uncluttering what is around you and inside you. When loss is sudden and violent, it is like a bomb exploded in your soul. Picking through the rubble takes time. It is like looking for all the broken pieces of your heart. Tears wash away ash and cleanse your sight, making the important things easier to see. Tears wash away the dust of the trivial, the toxic, the temporary. What remains is treasure.[2]

In my first months of grief, much of what I was feeling can be described as despair. It is a drastic word, but on one level it can be a good place for a child of God to be. Despair means to lose all hope or confidence. For me to despair meant that I recognized my inability to fix my broken heart. Despair drove me to the heart of God, because human resources were worthless. The book of Hebrews is written to people like me, people who longed for what was. People terrified of the future. Throughout this book, the writer confronts the readers' fears by reminding them of the past faithfulness of God and the confidence they can have in his presence. Like me, they struggled to reconcile their circumstances with their preconceived notions of God's plans. If God was good, always good, then why were Christians facing martyrdom? Why wasn't his church victorious? The writer reminds them once again of the supremacy of Christ: "In putting everything under him, God left nothing that is not subject to him. Yet at present we do not see everything subject to him. But we see Jesus" (Heb. 2:8b–9a).

A friend reminded me of this simple truth when she gave us a plaque that reads: "You never know that Jesus is all you need until Jesus is all you have."

The black blanket of despair is the perfect backdrop for the glow of Christ's love. Tears of despair drove me to the foot of the cross where I cried out, "O God, if you do not meet me in the darkness, I will not survive. You must come to me. You must!" It was in the midnight darkness I learned to whisper, "But I see Jesus!"

Tears of despair slowly opened my eyes to the sufficiency of Jesus.

TREASURES OF HOPE

Scriptural Gems

"Let us fix our eyes on Jesus, the author and perfecter of our faith." (Heb. 12:2)

> "I am worn out from groaning;
>   all night long I flood my bed with weeping
>   and drench my couch with tears.
> My eyes grow weak with sorrow;
>   they fail because of all my foes.
> Away from me, all you who do evil,
>   for the LORD has heard my weeping.
> The LORD has heard my cry for mercy." (Ps. 6:6–9)

"He who watches over you . . . will neither slumber nor sleep." (Ps. 121:3–4)

"During the days of Jesus' life on earth, he offered up prayers and petitions with loud cries and tears to the one who could save him from death, and he was heard because of his reverent submission. Although he was a son, he learned obedience from what he suffered and, once made perfect, he became the source of eternal salvation for all who obey him." (Heb. 5:7–9)

"He is . . . a man of sorrows and acquainted with grief." (Isa. 53:3 KJV)

"[At the death of Lazarus] Jesus wept. Then the Jews said, 'See how he loved him!' But some of them said, 'Could not he who opened the eyes of the blind man have kept this man from dying?' " (John 11:35–37)

Sometimes God's Word may taste like dry toast, but I encourage you to keep going back to Scripture as your guidebook for this painful journey. If you don't know where to start in the Bible, read the Scriptures cited above in my journal entries, as well as the following Scriptures, from Psalm 86, which I responded to in other July 1993 journal entries. In your journal, record your response.

> Teach me your way, O LORD, and I will walk in your truth; give me an undivided heart. (Ps. 86:11)

> For great is your love toward me; you have delivered my soul from the depths of the grave. (Ps. 86:13)

> Give me a sign of your goodness, that my enemies [such as death, sorrow, doubts, if onlys] may see it and be put to shame, for you, O LORD, have helped me and comforted me. (Ps. 86:17)

Songs in the Night: What a Friend We Have in Jesus
As a child I sat with my parents and grandmother in our tiny Presbyterian church and gustily sang the old hymns as though I

understood and believed every word. Did I have any idea what
griefs and *trials* could mean? Only in my sorrow could I make
this song the prayer of my ravaged heart. What does it say to you
about hope?

> What a Friend we have in Jesus, all our sins and griefs
>   to bear!
> What a privilege to carry ev'rything to God in prayer!
> O what peace we often forfeit, O what needless pain
>   we bear,
> All because we do not carry ev'rything to God in
>   prayer.
>
> Have we trials and temptations? Is there trouble any-
>   where?
> We should never be discouraged: take it to the Lord in
>   prayer!
> Can we find a friend so faithful, who will all our sor-
>   rows share?
> Jesus knows our ev'ry weakness—take it to the Lord in
>   prayer!
>
> Are we weak and heavy-laden, cumbered with a load of
>   care?
> Precious Savior, still our refuge—take it to the Lord in
>   prayer!
> Do thy friends despise, forsake thee? Take it to the Lord
>   in prayer;
> In his arms he'll take and shield thee; thou wilt find a
>   solace there.

This hymn means even more to me now that I know the
story behind it. Irishman Joseph Scriven planned to marry his

sweetheart and build a Christian home and business. But the day before the wedding, his fiancée drowned. He moved to Canada—where he helped the poor in an attempt to forget his grief—and there a second fiancée died, of pneumonia. Soon after, he wrote this comforting poem for his mother. She must have sent it to friends, who sent it to a Christian periodical where it was published with no attribution. In time, the original copy was discovered by a neighbor in Mr. Scrivin's sickroom. Perhaps God will lead you to write a poem or a prayer that will comfort others.

Other Hopeful Ideas

How do you respond to the following quote by Dante: "I wept not, so of stone grew I within"?

Journal your response to the following—a portion of a nineteenth-century letter of consolation written by Charles Kingsley: "Perhaps sorrow is sent that we may give way to it, and in drinking the cup to the dregs, find some medicine in it itself which we should not find if we began doctoring ourselves. . . . If we say simply, 'I am wretched—I ought to be wretched'; then we shall perhaps hear a voice: 'Who made thee wretched but God? Then what can he mean but thy good?' And if the heart answers impatiently: 'My good? I don't want it, I want my love,' perhaps the voice may answer, 'Then thou shalt have both in time.' "[3]

Two thousand years ago Egyptian and Middle Eastern artisans captured the symbolism of David's cry to God in Psalm 56:8, "put thou my tears in thy bottle, are they not written in thy book?" They created small, exquisite glass bottles for mourners to fill with their tears. In Roman times the bereaved placed their full tear bottles in burial tombs to demonstrate their love and respect for the departed loved one. Ornately decorated silver and pewter bottles reappeared during the nineteenth century. When the tears collected in the tiny bottles evaporated, their mourning season was over. David's words evoke a picture of God lovingly catching my tears and placing them in a precious crystal bottle as a reminder that he is well aware of my sorrow and notices every tear.

Perhaps these little bottles are reappearing in antique and Christian bookstores because of the ever-widening circle of grief that grips our world. You might try to find one for your tears.

Anticipate that tears will flow at unexpected moments. If you are in a public setting in the presence of others, ask them to give you a minute, step aside, get a drink of water, take several deep breaths, and ask God for extra strength. Go for a walk around your office building or your yard. If you can't gain control, go to a private place and just cry.

Ask God to draw you to one short Scripture phrase or verse— or possibly a hymn phrase—that you might repeat to yourself in your most emotionally despairing moments. It might be as basic as the description of God given by Paul in 2 Corinthians 1:3: "the God of all comfort" ("who comforts us in all our troubles"). Or 2 Corinthians 1:19: "God is faithful." (You might read and find strength in all of 2 Cor. 1.)

Prayer: The Jewel of Tears

Father, thank you for the jewel of tears and your permission to grieve honestly—that you invite us to come into your presence with our questions and doubts. We wait for you to keep your promises of comfort and wisdom.

6

WRESTLING TO REST

THE TREASURE OF TRUST

 MIDNIGHT PRINCIPLE: God's grace is not an anesthetic.

JOURNAL INSIGHT

July 16. Please help me trust you again. You are leading me to the story of Job.

Job 1:1–5. Job's family was obviously a close one. They often had each other over. Job prayed for his children regularly, because he feared they may have had sin in their hearts.

Job 1:20. With your permission, Satan takes everything from Job, including his ten children. Job falls to the ground and worships.

Job 2:10. After Job's wife urges him to curse God and die, Job asks, "Shall we accept good from God and not trouble [also]?"

We hear so much about the patience of Job, but I don't see it. What I see is a broken-hearted man striving to trust the One who is sovereign over every detail of his life, the One who could have stopped these horrific events from stripping Job of everything and everyone. After describing some of the mysteries and pains of life, he exclaims the very words that express my own soul: "What I feared has come upon me. What I dreaded has happened to me. I have no peace, no quietness: I have no rest, but only turmoil" (Job 3:25–26).

Thank you, Job, for your honest response to horrific circumstances.

This holy man is in a battle, a wrestling match with the purpose of understanding the character of his God. He doesn't blame Satan. He cries out to you, God! In Job 5:18, he proclaims, "For he wounds, but he also binds us; he injures, but his hands also heal." Job clearly is trying to reconcile your love with your sovereign care. He wants to trust you, but he is confused, mystified.

His friends try to comfort him with faulty theology. For their own sakes, they must explain Job's pain. They must blame him for it, because then they can protect their definition of your character and thus maintain control over you and their lives. They have lived believing that they can control you by being good. Job's circumstances are like a wind that blows down their carefully crafted house of cards. . . . Job's friends believe that if they are good, you owe them; you are obligated to keep them and all their loved ones safe and healthy and wealthy. In other words, they can control you if only they are good enough, if they have enough faith. But isn't that the obvious hole in their theology? We can't be good enough. The only hope we have for goodness is being washed clean in the blood of your own beloved son, Jesus.

Job 6:1–10. Job isn't buying into their definition of God. He refuses to believe that his personal sin brought on these calamities. He despairs of life: "Oh, that I might have my request, that God would grant my hope. I wish he would crush me. I wish he would reach out his hand and kill me" (6:8–9, NLT).

I gain hope from Job, because then he declares, "At least I can take comfort in this: Despite the pain, I have not denied the words of the Holy One" (6:10 NLT).

And yet, I wonder if Job longs for death, even while not denying God's faithfulness

O God, I know I am a sinner. I know that I don't deserve any blessings; all of my righteousness is as a "filthy rag" (Isa. 64:6). Only Jesus is righteous. But like Job, I am confident that I have served you as best I know how, serving you in the context of your grace and the righteousness of Christ, depending on the comfort of your seeing me as position- ally pure, because you chose me to be your daughter for rea- sons I cannot fathom. I have lived in the absolute certainty that there is nothing that can separate me from your love. I will never believe that you took Mark because of our sin or his sin. All I have to do is look around at other families where the parents don't care about their children. I see teens who blatantly rebel and sin, still alive. . . . Mark was a sinner, of course, but he did not drink or use drugs. He served you in the church, he was loved by his friends and family. We knew where he was all the time. So, with Job, I can say that you did not take Mark because of our personal sin or his.

I know why you took Mark. I don't even have to ask why. Jesus answered the question when asked why a particular man was born blind: "Rabbi, who sinned, this man or his par- ents, that he was born blind?"

"Neither this man nor his parents sinned," said Jesus, "but this happened so that the work of God might be displayed in his life" (John 9:2–3).

Mark's death is an opportunity for your glory to be dis- played. I am too weak for this assignment. . . .

We live in a broken world. Original sin has its consequences. The rain falls on the just and the unjust alike. Believers and unbelievers lose their children, suffer from disease, catastrophe. What is the difference you expect? That your children will deepen in their trust in you. That we will see that everything we have is on loan from you, especially our children. Your plan is to redeem the pain of our loss and use it for eternal purposes. I wish I were spiritual enough to say that I am thankful to be a part of your eternal plan in this way, that I will search out ways to partner with you in this eternal plan. But I'm not there, Lord. And I don't know if I ever will be. I want my child back. You are God. You don't need my child to build your kingdom. You gave your own Son; He is enough. What are you doing with our child? Children bury their elderly parents; parents should not have to bury their children. Lord, where is the love? I would never wound my child the way you have wounded us, your children. What loving Father performs surgery without anesthetic? Your grace is not an anesthetic. How can I trust you again? What difference does righteousness make? What difference does it make how we raise our children; how we try to protect them? How do I know you won't take another one? Lord, even as I write these words a tiny part of me is saying, "Sharon, be careful. You know you don't mean those words."

But in this second, this instance, I do mean those words. Maybe I am asking why. Yet even in my ugliness, your mercy calls me. When I am weak, you promise to be strong (2 Cor. 12:10). You are reminding me of Scriptures I memorized as a child and you are forcing me to make a choice. Will I trust you again?

Lamentations 3:19–24: "I remember my affliction and my wandering, the bitterness and the gall. I well remember them, and my soul is downcast within me. Yet this I call to mind and therefore I have hope: Because of the Lord's great love we are not consumed, for his compassions never fail. They are new every morning; great is your faithfulness. I say to myself, 'The Lord is my portion; therefore I will wait for him.' "

STRUGGLING TO SURRENDER

Struggling with Whom?

This long journal entry set the stage for weeks, months, of wrestling with God's purposes. Sometimes, to learn a lesson, we have to keep tackling an issue over and over again, each time gaining new, deeper understanding.

This was true in my parenting. For a long time, every time the phone rang or our children left our home my heart pounded with fear. We looked for ways to narrow the circle of fear; for example, all of us started carrying cell phones. One night when Dan left for a date, Chuck and I hovered over him, reminding him of what he already knew. He looked at me and asked, "We're starting over again, aren't we, Mom?" I tried not to cry as I nodded and said, "Yes, Dan, please be patient with me as I learn how to trust God with you." In my heart I whispered, *And, Lord, you and I are starting over again, aren't we? Please be patient with me.*

July 31. Dear Father, the idea of wrestling with you in order to rest in you is foreign to me. Yet I can't pretend I trust you or that I surrender easily to the pathway you have marked out for me. Grappling with you is risky. But I am learning I'm in good company. Scriptures honestly recount the stories of others who struggled to reconcile their circumstances with your character. And in the darkness you came to each one. Sarah and her daughter-in-law Rebekah both cried out from the abyss of infertility. Hannah, too, came to you with her tear-covered longing for a child. Weary, empty Elijah raged against his supposed aloneness, and you gave him food, rest, and hope. Fearful Jacob ran to you as his brother's army marched toward him. Moses argued with you about his ability to do what you commanded.

People in Scripture who struggled to walk by faith knew that their struggle was with you, not Satan. Even Job. When Job protested his losses, he didn't say, "The Lord gave and the devil took it all away!" No, he exclaimed that you took it all away. But somehow he also knew that you are not the author of evil. This is so hard.

You commissioned Jeremiah, the weeping prophet, for a terrible job. He had to give a harsh and bitter message to his countrymen. Poor Jeremiah. He was ostracized, threatened with death by his own people, thrown into prison, tried for his life by the priests, locked in stocks, thrown into a cistern, publicly humiliated, not permitted to marry. He cried out to you, "Lord, what's going on here?" His struggle was not with the people rejecting the message. His struggle was with you.

And then in the Garden of Gethsemane, the night before the crucifixion, Jesus cried out to you, "Father, if there is another way. . . ." Three times your Son pleaded, "If it is possible, let this cup pass from me." But then he surrendered, "Father, if you are willing, take this cup from me; yet not my will, but yours be done" (Luke 22:42).

Jesus was wrestling with you, his Father. In his wrestling is the heart of surrender, not a raised fist, not a waggling finger in your face. He "learned obedience from what he suffered" (Heb. 5:8). Who can understand this?

I don't know how to surrender. Please help me.

Naming a Fear

A few days later, after a wrenching cry, I sensed the Lord speaking Scripture to my spirit: "Sharon, in quietness and trust shall be your strength" (Isa. 30:15). My journal in response to this identifies one of the fears I had to overcome before I could move to the next level of surrender.

August 3. To trust is to surrender. Does surrendering to your grace mean that I'm letting go of Mark? If I surrender, am I saying, "It's OK, Lord. You took my son, and I don't miss him anymore"? . . . How can I ever experience joy without abandoning Mark?

I don't like the words *letting go of Mark*. How can I let go of someone who has already gone? And I bet that like me you hate the words *it's time to move on*. To move on requires leaving a loved one behind. Our grief keeps us connected to the one we love so much. But it also fills up places in our souls in such a way that there is no room for other treasures. Casting the burden of our sorrow onto the strong shoulders of our heavenly Father lightens our load, making room for joy to seep in. Such surrender is not an over-and-done-with decision. It is a long, hard process that must be repeated again and again because every day your heart will discover a new reason for grieving.

The Command and the Choice

Frederick Buechner once said, "To be commanded to love God at all, let alone in the wilderness, is like being commanded to be well when we are sick, to sing for joy when we're dying of thirst, to run when our legs are broken. But this is the first and great commandment nonetheless. Even in the wilderness, especially in the wilderness—you shall love him."

I thought I loved God before July 6. In the wilderness of death I learned that sometimes loving him is not a feeling, it's a choice. Every minute I wearily struggled to choose to obey his command to love him. Sometimes he gave me a treasure in the darkness that was a respite from the hard work of grief and a sign of his intimate knowledge of the needs of my soul.

The day after I named my fear of abandoning Mark, Melanie and my two dear friends, Diane and Brenda, helped me clean out Mark's room. Letting go of Mark required stages, so I planned to identify items for each of our kids to keep and box up the rest of his things for sorting through later.

August 4. My sister Jane Anne called to pray with me before we started. Later she told me that Joan called her, and they prayed together for me. Joan specifically prayed that you, Lord, would give me a sign of your presence— that we would find something that would help me trust you, something from Mark. I would have thought this a useless request, because the kids had already gone through Mark's personal belongings, searching for insights into his heart and mind. But you hid from them what would mean the most to his parents.

The kids did not find his prayer journal, we did. More than two years ago Chuck gave each of the boys a notebook and assigned specific Proverbs to study each week. He asked them to record their thoughts as prayers. You saved this treasure for me to find. His handwriting. His prayers. His struggles. Simple, written by a young teen. An honest reflection into Mark's heart and longing to be righteous. Salty tears splashed on the pages as I read an entry from spring 1991:

I recommitted my life to Christ and have tried to live up to it since then. It is not easy to give up all the temptations, but it is something that I have got to do. My weakness is without a doubt the temptations that come back to me after I decided to change. . . . There is no way that I can withstand the temptations by myself so I know that I can turn to God . . . I know that if the sky were to fall on my head right now, I would stand before God and he would let me into his kingdom. I know that I do not deserve it, but I know that God is a God full of mercy, and he says that if I ask then he will come in and that is enough for me.

O Father, thank you for this affirmation of a boyish faith, a sign that you exist, that you hear prayers. May your word be enough for me, too.

Mark's description of his struggle to fight temptation resonated with my own struggle to surrender to God's purposes. Melanie, Diane, Brenda, and I joined hands and thanked God for giving us this gift. Finding Mark's prayer journal after days of begging God for pain relief was confirmation that in the darkness were treasures designed by the Creator God to meet intimate needs in my heart that only he understood. Reading Mark's words was like hearing a bell that signaled the end of this round of wrestling. This treasure broke the ache for a few hours.

Mark's journal was like a greeting card from God with the words, "I am all powerful but always present with my children. I am all knowing of every detail of your life. The number of hairs on your head changes every minute but at all times I know how many are there. I am the Creator God and yet when a sparrow falls, I'm there. Sharon, revealing Mark's journal is what you needed at this very moment to help you surrender your son to my purposes. Now rest from your struggles for a while and let me love you."

Lord, Will You Guide Us?

In mid-August our family traveled to the Outer Banks for a vacation and extended-family reunion. I'll talk about this vacation more in the next chapter. For now I want to illustrate how our entire extended family was wrestling, the young as well as the old.

I have six siblings and more than fifty nieces and nephews. All of them were there, all of them without any experience or instruction on how to respond to the loss of a young family member. Because Chuck was a pastor, family members often turned to him in times of crisis. Now he was helpless to help himself, let alone help anyone else. We were little ships trying to navigate a raging storm. We had no instruction manual, no maps. Some of the children were better than their parents at putting into words our confusion.

We all held our breath and stopped talking when four-year-old Rachel Mae nonchalantly asked, "Aunt Sharon, why did your big Mark get in an accident and die? Why did he?"

"I don't know, Rachel."

"But why did he?"

"Because God wanted him to go to heaven."

"But why?"

"Rachel, I don't know why. But whenever you see me crying, you'll know it's because I miss Mark, and that's when I need a hug."

Silence.

"Aunt Sharon, why do you paint your toe nails?"

Oh, to have such childlike faith and acceptance of the answers that God gives to me. Why can't I just accept your call: "Sharon, trust me. Your child is safe with me." Why can't I just trust, God?

Another conversation—ten-year-old Elizabeth Jane to her mother, Jane Anne: "I've been thinking a lot since Mark died. It doesn't really matter if we pray. God does what he wants. It doesn't make much sense to pray. Why should we?"

Jane Anne to Elizabeth: "All I know is Jesus needed to pray when he was on earth. If he needed to pray, so do we."

Elizabeth to Jane Anne: "Five people I love have died. That's enough."

Nina and Jim's kids: "Mom, everyone we prayed for has died."

Rachel Mae: "Aunt Sharon, someday we will all die and go to heaven and be with your big Mark and we won't be sad anymore."

Lord, you've rocked all of us.

On that vacation my mother finished reading *Roses in December* by Marilyn Heavilin.[1] She told me she'd given the book to my father and told him he had to read it, "because it explains the way you are grieving; it is totally opposite of what we would do, but it is right for you. And we need to understand."

I am grateful that she is trying to help us by studying us and reading the books we are reading. She was raised to be a stoic in the face of loss: Do not cry in the presence of the bereaved; do not mention the name of the child; go on with life. Be normal. She knows this is not the right way for us. We are all in a strange, terrifying country. We need a guide. Lord, will you guide us?

The Promise of God's Presence

The promise of God's presence became a pinpoint of guiding light that slowly led me into his heart. Every time someone like Moses, Joshua, Gideon, or Jeremiah responded to God's call with the words, "I'm just a child. I don't know how to speak. I can't do this," God didn't say, "Buck up, pull yourself up by your own boot straps; if you have enough faith, I'll make it easy for you, give you what you want." No. God replied with words so simple, so easy to understand and yet so difficult to trust. "I will never leave or forsake you. Don't be afraid."[2]

Ultimately that was the message I clung to, even as I continued my journey of grief.

THE TREASURE OF WRESTLING

"But sir," Gideon replied, "if the LORD is with us, why has all this happened to us? Where are all of his wonders that our fathers told us about when they said, 'Did not the LORD bring us up out of Egypt?' But now the LORD has abandoned us and put us into the hand of Midian."

The LORD turned to him and said, "Go in the strength you have and save Israel out of Midian's hand. Am I not sending you? . . . I will be with you." (Judg. 6:13–14, 16)

Instead of giving me the riches of serene peace, God gave me the jewel of wrestling, a treasure that seemed more like a worthless bauble than a precious gem. It has taken a long time to realize God gave me exactly what I needed.

Should you wrestle before God? What if you go too far? What if you stay in the wrestling ring or use my experience as an excuse to stay wrapped up in bitterness and rage? I am afraid to write these things because you may misinterpret them. Yet I have concluded that every believer should wrestle before God or risk staying stuck in dry orthodoxy.

It was a long time before my wrestling led to resting. And it was even longer before wrestling revealed how extending God's mercy to others would help redeem the pain of losing our son.

Grappling with God's truth enabled me to come to a point where I concluded, "Your ways don't make sense, but I am choosing to trust you because you have demonstrated your love for me in ways I can never understand."

You may have run into those who exhort, "Your tears and long-term grief indicate weak faith and small love for God. God loves you. He is good all the time. Why can't you just trust him?"

Before July 6, I trusted God with all of life. I trusted him to take care of my child. I knew that he never promised life would be easy. But the deaths of Mark and his friend felt like a betrayal of a covenant bond. How could this be love? Honestly confronting this question was the only means for me to find a reason to get up in the morning and have purpose in life. If God is not involved in these circumstances, then Mark's death is an accident that just happened. And all of my questions and cries fall on the ears of no one; after I wail and scream, my only option is resignation to a purposeless life where no one with any wisdom has any control. But if I have a personal relationship with God, Someone who is perfectly wise and loving is listening. And that gives me hope.

In his wonderful book *If God Is So Good, Why Do I Hurt So Bad?* David Biebel helped me understand why intimacy with God initially made my pathway to healing more difficult:

Faith makes the process personal. And although this does hold promise for resolution as opposed to resignation, for a while things can become quite bewildering.

The pain may intensify. Beyond the loss that brought me here is the pain of knowing it is from the Father's hand. He may not have caused it, true, but He certainly must have allowed it. He could have intervened. Why did it have to happen this way? Why did it have to happen to us?

The confusion may compound. How can this be love? And how can I love Him, if this is what I get for it? Not only must I be reconciled with some unacceptable event, but I must also be reconciled with the One I hold responsible.[3]

The conflicted feelings I had were at times terrifying, leading me to believe I might be losing my mind. One of the most freeing remarks Marilyn Heavilin said to me in our phone conversation was, "What you are experiencing is *normal*. Mark's death is forcing you to find and live with a new level of normal."

David Biebel goes on to confirm this conclusion:

This kind of confusion is *normal* for people struggling with loss, especially believers. Remember, others can just walk away, their protests dissipating into an apparently heartless universe.

But you—you believe that God loves you, and that in everything he causes or allows he is motivated by that love, and that as your heavenly Father, He has in mind only what will ultimately be for your best. Reconciling these paradoxical ideas may take some time, perhaps a long, long time.[4]

Perhaps one of the most difficult issues initially was that every other problem in my life had a solution, a moment when it would be over. In other words, I or someone I loved could fix it. I wrote in my journal that maybe if I started screaming and screaming that someone would understand I couldn't face life with this sorrow. And they would give me back Mark. In my mind I knew that was not an option. In my heart I clung to the possibility. I begged God to explain so that I could let go and trust only him. He used Hebrews 11:13–16 as an anti-inflammatory medication. God will keep all of his promises, but he would save some of those treasures for when I arrived in heaven. "All these people were still living by faith when they died. They did not receive the things promised; they only saw them and welcomed them from a distance" (Heb. 11:13).

To experience joy once more, I would have to learn to accept that God's thoughts are not my thoughts and his ways are not my ways (Isa. 55:8). Joy requires that I not only accept that truth but believe it is a good truth.

As I said earlier, the year we were married, Chuck and I chose a life verse: "But seek first his kingdom and his righteousness, and all these things will be given to you as well" (Matt. 6:33). I can't say the road has been easy, but I want to give you the hope of knowing that as I, through the power of the Spirit, chose to submit to God—even as I railed and wept and asked questions—and chose to take the next step in obedience, he has been faithful.

Note this quote by novelist George Eliot: "She was no longer wrestling with her grief, but could sit down with it as a lasting companion and make it a sharer in her thoughts."

Ten years after Mark's death, I can honestly change Eliot's words to read: Sharon is no longer wrestling with God, but instead can sit down with her heavenly Father as a lasting companion and recognize him as a sharer and shaper of her thoughts.

I pray that you too will wrestle to rest, maybe not soon and in one quick step and blow, but in God's good time.

TREASURES OF HOPE

Scriptural Gems

"Blessed is she who has believed that what the Lord has said to her will be accomplished!" (Luke 1:45)

"So then, those who suffer according to God's will should commit themselves to their faithful Creator and continue to do good." (1 Peter 4:19)

"Be very careful, then how you live—not as unwise but as wise, making the most of every opportunity, because the days are evil." (Eph. 5:15)

"Christ Jesus . . . has destroyed death and has brought life and immortality to light through the gospel." (2 Tim. 1:10)

"The righteous perish, and no one ponders it in his heart; devout men are taken away, and no one understands that the righteous are taken away to be spared from evil. Those who walk uprightly enter into peace; they find rest as they lie in death." (Isa. 57:1–2)

"His divine power has given us everything we need for life and godliness through our knowledge of him who called us by his own glory and goodness." (2 Peter 1:3)

At the beginning of the chapter I shared a journal entry that included Scriptures from the beginning of Job's story. Consider these jewels from later in the book of Job:

- God is kind and watches over me: "You gave me life and showed me kindness, and in your providence watched over my spirit." (Job 10:12)
- My life is not an accident: "I know that you can do all things; no plan of yours can be thwarted." (Job 42:2)
- God is in control: "But he knows the way that I take; when he has tested me, I will come forth as gold." (Job 23:10)
- My life is not a surprise to God: "Does he not see my ways and count my every step?" (Job 31:4)
- God will save me: "I know that my Redeemer lives, and that in the end he will stand upon the earth." (Job 19:25)

Songs in the Night: I Need Thee Every Hour

When grief stole my ability to articulate my heart, I wrote out hymns as prayers to God. If this simple hymn touches your heart the way it has mine, write out the words in your journal as an intimate prayer to God.

> I need thee ev'ry hour, most gracious Lord;
> No tender voice like thine can peace afford.
>
> I need thee ev'ry hour; stay thou nearby;
> Temptations lose their pow'r when thou art nigh.
>
> I need thee ev'ry hour, in joy or pain;
> Come quickly, and abide, or life is vain.
>
> I need thee ev'ry hour; teach me thy will,
> And thy rich promises in me fulfill.
>
> I need thee ev'ry hour, Most Holy One;
> O make me thine indeed, thou blessed Son.

[Refrain]
I need thee, O I need thee,
Ev'ry hour I need thee;
O bless me now, my Savior, I come to thee.

Other Hopeful Ideas

In his love for us, God in Scripture does not hide the frailty of his children. For that reason, the book of Psalms is a special place of comfort for wrestling believers. By including these accounts in his Word, God affirms our need to ask questions and go directly to his heart with our doubts, anger, and need for clarification. Many of these passages reverberate with the cries of Jesus in the Garden of Gethsemane just before the crucifixion. Pull out your journal and Bible and ask God to open your heart and eyes to one aspect of his truth as you struggle to reconcile your circumstances with his love.

Slowly read Psalm 77. Note the phrases that best describe your response to your loss. Read it out loud and personalize it by replacing all personal pronouns with your name. Write out how you feel when you read the psalmist's conclusions about God's character and faithfulness.

Mary, the mother of Jesus, immediately surrendered to the announcement that she, a virgin, would bear the Messiah. Read her song (Luke 1:46–56) and note what she says about the character of God. How does your loss affect your view of the character of God?

Even as you wrestle, I encourage you to live as you claim to believe. Do you believe that you are in God's grip? If God is telling the truth, and he has to be because he cannot lie (Num. 23:18), then he is holding you tightly in his grip (John 10:27–28). Practice living in that grip.

Do you believe that God is with you right now and will never leave or forsake you? Recognize the commandment of God in Joshua 1:9 and practice living in his presence: "Have I not commanded you? Be strong and courageous. Do not be terrified; do not be discouraged, for the LORD your God will be with you wherever you go."

Prayer: Light after Darkness

Shortly after Mark's death, by faith, I wrote this hymn by Frances Ridley Havergal as a prayer. Write it out in your journal as a declaration of your hope in God's promises of his presence, comfort, and eternal healing.

Father,

Light after darkness. Gain after loss.

Strength after weakness. Crown after cross.

Sweet after bitter. Hope after fears.

Home after wandering. Praise after tears. Amen.

7

ECHOES OF MERCY

THE TREASURE OF COMFORTING MESSAGES

 **MIDNIGHT PRINCIPLE:** When midnight darkness falls, listen and watch closely; you may hear and see things that you don't normally experience.

JOURNAL INSIGHT

August 19, 1993. We are on vacation in Duck, North Carolina. Mark's favorite place. We have stayed in the same house for the past several years. Lots of fun memories, and now lots of pain. We are here because Daniel insisted that he needed to come to feel close to Mark. To revisit their special haunts. But being here is torture for Chuck and me. And I think Daniel is wondering if we should have come. But this morning you rang a bell that signaled the end of this round of wrestling. The short respite gave me a chance to catch my breath and choose to enjoy remembering the joy of caring for my family.

Today Daniel had an early morning surfing session. When he got back, he asked, "Mom, can you fix me a big breakfast with French toast?" His request startled me; at first I didn't want to do it. Then I saw the twinkle in his eyes and recognized a private message. I smiled back as I pictured the boys and their friends coming in from early morning surf sessions, ravenous, anticipating the hot piles of pancakes or French toast. I prepared Daniel's breakfast with gratitude for the privilege of demonstrating my love for this son rather than grieving the inability to serve both boys. As I watched Daniel enjoying his food, I wondered why he seemed so at ease. Slowly he explained. When he and Mark would surf together and one of them caught a great wave, the other would belt out a special yell. This morning, after he caught a big wave, he thought he heard Mark yell for him. He sheepishly added that it was probably just someone on the shore, but it sounded just like their special way of communicating. In his soul, Daniel thinks it was Mark. So do I.

LITTLE IS MUCH

The angry words spewed out of the young woman. "My baby died. The treasures God gives should equal that sorrow. I need more than my husband's smile or a flower to make me feel better."

I understood her rage.

In the fresh waves of grief, I wanted physical signs that God was present. With the psalmist I prayed, "Give me a sign of your goodness, that my enemies may see it and be put to shame, for you, O LORD, have helped me and comforted me" (Ps. 86:17). Of course the problem with my prayer was that I defined for God what the sign had to be. Every time I stepped outside I looked up into the sky, hoping for a cloud formation that declared, "Sharon, Mark is fine! He's with me!" I reasoned that the treasures in darkness promised by God should equal the enormity of the loss.

When none of that happened, I searched for academic answers to life's questions. I eagerly grabbed at any tidbit that seemed to help me make sense out of God. But just as soon as I organized my belief system, waves of sorrow shattered my carefully reasoned conclusions.

Ultimately I had to accept that faith is not based on circumstances, emotions, logic, or experiences. It's trust that God is God. His Word is true because he is true. It's a matter of the heart.

But in the beginning of my sorrow, God condescended to my immature, frail faith. His treasures taught me that he speaks through his still, small voice, and the midnights of our lives can make us especially aware of that voice. It's risky to share with others these special gifts of God because many people place experience above God's Word. But in our quest to be doctrinally correct, I think that sometimes we fear the intimacy that God promises through a personal relationship with his Son, Jesus. Of all people, those who hold to the doctrines of grace should experience the most intimacy with our Redeemer God.

In God's eternal economy, little is much when he is in it. David slew Goliath with one smooth stone (1 Sam. 17). One cloud ended a drought in the days of Elijah (1 Kings 17–18).

Jesus fed thousands with five little loaves of bread and two fish (Matt. 13:14–21). The disciples tried to shoo away the children, and Jesus rebuked them: "Let the little children come to me, and do not hinder them, for the kingdom of heaven belongs to such as these" (Matt. 19:14). And many of us remember Jesus teaching us that faith as small as a grain of mustard seed can move mountains (Matt. 17:20).

Priceless gifts often come in tiny packages. When I least expected his treasures in the darkness, he sent them—wrapped up in grace. He designed each one to remind me that he is the Lord my God, the One who calls me by name (Isa. 45:2–3).

A *Still, Small Voice*

Chuck closed one of his messages with words that helped me discern whether some not-easily explainable experiences in the summer and fall of 1993 were meant as comforting messages to us from God:

> Sudden pain can be incredibly self-centered. We demand that God do things our way—fix us according to our plan! But sometimes he doesn't seem to be listening. Remember: God is present even when he seems to be deaf or appears to have taken an extended leave of absence. God's timing is perfect, even when it appears he is late. For reasons that are impossible to explain, we human beings are precious to God and we must choose to remember that even when we don't feel his love.
>
> Our source of comfort must be his Word. However, the veil between this world and the next is gossamer thin for broken people. Sometimes God gives us special touches like a star that falls at just the moment you requested a physical demonstration of his presence. But he will never, never do anything that is against his Word

or lead you away from trusting him alone. Someone has said that the night has a thousand eyes, while the day has only one. In the midnights of life, watch carefully and listen for his still small voice.[1]

Then he told them about the evidences of his presence we experienced on our vacation.

Keeper of the Stars

August 1993. North Carolina. O God, you are so "wholly other," so distant, so big, so far away. The God of creation. Yet you are ever-present, close by, touching my soul, binding up my wounded heart. How can you be both?

Psalm 147:3–4: "He heals the brokenhearted and binds up their wounds. He determines the number of the stars and calls them each by name."

Last night as we sat on the deck with Jim and Nina, we talked quietly about the past few weeks. After they left Chuck and I embraced and looked up at the stars. I didn't tell Chuck, but Lord, you know what I was thinking. "If only I could ask for a sign. Throw down a star. Lord, let me know by that falling star, falling at just that instance, that Mark is close by." I didn't ask for that sign because I _know_ you don't do things like that! Right? And if you didn't do what I asked, then I would have one more reason to suspect your presence. Just then the kids came up from the beach. Young

Chuck hesitated before speaking, "We were sitting on two different blankets. Melanie and I were talking about the possibility that each star represents a child of God in heaven. After all, God told Abraham that his descendants would number the stars! Dan, Mandy, Jill, and Chrisalyn were on another blanket saying the same things! Dan pointed out a blinking star and said that it might be Mark's. Suddenly, we all saw a bright, large shooting star that crossed the whole sky. I don't want to make too big a deal of all this, but Dad, would God do something like that as a sign of his glory and control?! To let us know that he heard us? It was like Mark heard our conversation and God gave him permission to let us know. . . ."

Chuck laughed and said, "Two months ago I might have been able to answer that question! I probably would have let you think it was a sign, but in my heart I would believe it was just a coincidence. Now, well, I just don't know. I am learning that the veil between this world and the next is gossamer thin." A few minutes later Chuck jumped up and stepped outside. Young Chuck looked at me, puzzled by his dad's exit. I smiled. "He's looking for his star." No sooner had I said it than he stepped back inside, wide eyed. "I just saw my star. It was like a ball of fire, and it went right over the house. It appeared to be skimming over the roof." He continued, "As I opened the door, I prayed, 'Give me a star. Show me your glory, Lord.' I looked up over the house rather than over the ocean, and there was this ball of fire streaking over the roof. I've never seen anything like it. It was so big and close I imagined I could have touched it."

This morning when I woke up, the enemy whispered, "The star was a coincidence. Lots of stars fall at this time of year. God doesn't care about you . . . even though he could send a star, he wouldn't. He's mean." Then I saw a little book on my dresser, written by grieving parents. Its title is your response to my doubts: Keeper of the Stars.

The title is like a gentle squeeze from you. "Sharon, ask me and watch what I can do!" I'm going to hold on to this treasure as a special blessing from you, an acknowledgment of our need for a special touch. You are the Keeper of the Stars, and you are the keeper of my heart.

Drummer Dreams

In the next six months, various family members heard other "echoes of mercy"—a phrase from the old, favorite gospel song "Blessed Assurance" by Fanny Crosby. In September young Chuck began having vivid dreams, even visions, of Mark playing his drums. He says,

> I would wake up in the middle of the night and "see" Mark playing the drums in my room. I can still see the angle of him playing—his body and the drums were out-

lined in white—a surreal vision. The first couple of times I wrote it off as hallucinations. The third, fourth, and tenth times I knew it was real. . . . This continued— not every night, just now and then. Then one night I also heard music, a song, even a genre, unlike any I have ever heard before. I believe I was hearing heavenly worship. I was wide awake watching and hearing this in my room at home. I grew scared as the music faded, and I began to cry, because I missed Mark. The reality of the situation was I wouldn't really be with and see my brother for fifty to sixty years if I lived a normal life. My brother wouldn't be at my wedding, be Uncle Mark to my kids, play on our softball teams, play drums on our worship team. . . . That was the reality of things. And it made me very sad."

There's a bit more to Chuck's story, which we'll share in the last chapter. But, as for the dreams, he says,

I believe God sometimes uses dreams and visions. Later on this was further confirmed when a friend of mine was praying, in a field behind her house. She was burdened for our family, and as she prayed looked up into the sky at the clouds. She was stunned when she "saw" Mark playing the drums. She rushed inside and drew a picture of what she'd seen. When I told her about my dream of Mark, she showed me her picture. It was *exactly* the same thing I had seen all those nights. If you know any- thing about drums, you'll appreciate he was sitting at the same angle, the same posture and approach to the drums—everything was exactly the same.

I know that many people who are wiser and smarter than I might roll their eyes at my story. And you may be thinking, You poor sap. Get real. A picture in the clouds? A dream? But nothing I saw is against God's Word. Mark is in heaven. He is worshiping God. It's easy for me to believe that God has perfected Mark's musical skills and that he is one of the great cloud of witnesses who are worshiping in heaven.

Love Letters from Mark

We received more messages of grace, echoes of mercy— some of them less dramatic than falling stars or dreams. One autumn evening I was restless and longing for Mark. Instead of curling up in a ball and crying, I felt led to organize my family mementos. Let me explain: If a child had touched it, I had saved it—all tucked into my bottom dresser drawer until I can get to it. Each cherished item—Heidi's coming home from the hospital little orange dress, matching shoes, and white organza hat, the boys' baptismal outfits, Mother's Day and Father's Day cards, birthday cards. Each one touched me with special memories.

But what was this? I recognized Mark's block handwriting. Butterflies fluttered in my stomach and tears flowed. My heart beat faster. My hands shook as I unfolded the pages. Could this really be? I began to read, "Mom, the best way that I can describe you would be 'the nagging mother'. . . . I thank God for the mom he has given me."

I smiled as I tried to remember the context; our children rarely remembered my birthday or Chuck's, because they were right after Christmas. More gifts felt like gluttony, and we did not encourage them to buy us more stuff. But in January 1993, Mark wrote us birthday letters. I did not remember this letter or what was in it, but God did, and he gave it to me at just the right moment.

The way that you nag always leaves me with another les- son learned. I don't think that I have ever done something wrong the second time without knowing it's not what I should be doing. Another characteristic that has taught me many lessons would be how organized you are. You have showed me over the years that I should never do anything unprepared. Every time that I get stuck because of not being organized, I always think, "I should have listened to Mom!" The way that you reach out to people and show love for them teaches me that I should do the same. I have never witnessed a time when you were so full of anger that you just blew up and screamed at someone. Now that is an example that I should follow. I thank God for the mom he has given me. The mom he has given me is full of love, patience, and self-control. He gave me a mom that I can look up to and someday marry a woman like you. I hope that I am blessed someday as much as our family has been blessed. I thank you, Mom, for all that you have given me and I love you very much!

Love, Mark

I chuckled and wondered who was this patient, loving, sweet-tempered but nagging mother who never lost her temper! I held the letter in my hands, tried to feel his warmth, imagined him writing. I wept because Mark would never know the joy of marriage on this earth. I would never hold his children. But joy mixed with sorrow. God had given me a love note from my son!

I dug deeper into the papers and found Mark's letter to Chuck and knew that God had given me the perfect Christmas gift for his father. Later, whenever the enemy tried to lead us down a pathway of regrets or self-imposed guilt, we remembered these priceless treasures prepared for us by our God in anticipation of our great need to hear from Mark. We longed for just one more conversation with our son. These letters were a voice from heaven, better than a message written in the clouds.

THE TREASURE OF COMFORTING MESSAGES

By day the LORD directs his love, at night his song is with me—a prayer to the God of my life. (Ps. 42:8)

Chuck has always been transparent in his preaching and teaching. He invites listeners to come along with him in his spiritual journey, whether it's struggling with specific sin or reveling in the love of God. He did not change in his approach when we lost our son. Most people who experience such sorrow can go to their place of work and intentionally put aside their theological struggle to reconcile God's love and sovereignty. Chuck's work as a pastor forced him to constantly engage his mind with the mind of God. One struggle was for him—as it is for all of us—to stay pure in his application of doctrine. Broken people are vulnerable to twisting Scripture to rationalize wrong responses to sorrow. Chuck describes his process of judging experience against doctrinal and biblical truth.

For over three decades I have remained faithful to the Word, teaching and preaching sound doctrine. The Reformed faith in particular has cost me dearly. I have taken stands that were unpopular with the experientialists and emotionalists who seemed to jettison all that is written for a fix of sensationalism. I certainly did not want to be accused of doing that. Yet when one is faced with death and dying for what seems to be "all day long," he is so much closer to that invisible wall that separates the physical world from the spiritual world. I sought nothing clearly forbidden in the

Word, such as communicating with the dead. I never talked to my departed son. Nor did I ever ask God to give me anything he clearly forbade, such as signs and wonders to prove his love. I offered no fleeces even though there seemed to be biblical precedent for doing so.

Yet things happened I could not explain and would not even share publicly for fear that I would stand accused of the very things I preached against. Yet no one could convince me that I was delusional or imagining things. My heart yearned to know the truth. So I tested the waters on others who had lost believing loved ones. One night I led a group of bereaved parents in a discussion of this very matter. After sharing with them one or two of the more innocuous and yet mysterious stories that happened to my family, I asked them questions, such as "How thin is your wall?" and "Are there stories similar to mine you want to share?" The response was an eerie silence. I cringed in my chair and reasoned that I had now let the cat out of the bag. Surely the word would spread that the preacher had doctrinally headed south in his unmanageable grief. But the silence was pierced as one by one similar stories were told. The fear was supplanted by faith as the tears began to flow.

The next day I feared I had opened a Pandora's box of heresy and finally called out for help. I needed a man who shared my theological frame of reference who would not be afraid to tell me the truth. A respected and gifted pastor-educator (one of the more brilliant minds in my denomination) known for his doctrinal acumen in the seminary setting agreed to meet with me and serve as a sounding board. As I sat across the table from him and begged for answers, I related to him story after story of the inexplicable and the supernatural. I told him that for three decades I counseled those who would sit at the bed of a dying loved one to "listen carefully. Your loved ones are closer to God's presence and to his eternal world than they are to ours. Listen closely, for you will hear him speak."

I expected a stern rebuke, but instead this is what he told me. "Chuck, you have asked God, no, begged God to heal your broken heart. You have asked him to give you only what he deems best for that healing. God has constructed for you a grief room. It has a doorknob on both sides. It is your private room with a free pass for you to enter it as often as necessary. In his great love he has condescended to give you treasures of encouragement in the darkness of your soul. You will not always need these divine manifestations. But for now you do. Give yourself permission to enter that room and then to emerge. Do not blaspheme him. Neither fear pounding on his chest. He can handle it. Plead with him as your sovereign Creator Redeemer. Those stories are gifts to you from a Father of love. Does he not promise that in his Word?"

We then discussed a variety of Scriptures that attest to a prayer-hearing, prayer-answering God who delights in surprising us with good and perfect gifts (James 1:17).

Those wondrous gifts have lessened as we progress along our grief journey. But there can be no doubt that in the same way Jesus emptied himself of all but love, so he condescends as he deems it right to heal the brokenhearted.

TREASURES OF HOPE

Scriptural Gems

"My sheep listen to my voice; I know them, and they follow me. I give them eternal life, and they shall never perish; no one can snatch them out of my hand." (John 10:27–28)

> "The LORD is my shepherd, I shall not be in want.
> He makes me lie down in green pastures,
> he leads me beside quiet waters,
> he restores my soul.
> He guides me in paths of righteousness
> for his name's sake.
> Even though I walk
> through the valley of the shadow of death,
> I will fear no evil,
> for you are with me;
> your rod and your staff,
> they comfort me." (Ps. 23:1–4)

"The LORD came and stood there, calling as at the other times, 'Samuel! Samuel!' Then Samuel said, 'Speak, for your servant is listening.' " (1 Sam. 3:10)

"The Lord said, 'Go out and stand on the mountain in the presence of the Lord, for the Lord is about to pass by.' Then a great and powerful wind tore the mountains apart and shattered the rocks before the Lord, but the Lord was not in the wind. After the wind there was an earthquake, but the Lord was not in the earthquake. After the earthquake came a fire, but the Lord was not in the fire. And after the fire came a gentle whisper. When Elijah heard it, he pulled his cloak over his face and went out and stood at the mouth of the cave.

Then a voice said to him, 'What are you doing here, Elijah?' "
(1 Kings 19:11–13)

"And afterward, I will pour out my Spirit on all people. Your sons and daughters will prophesy, your old men will dream dreams, your young men will see visions." (Joel 2:28)

Songs in the Night: Spirit of God, Descend upon My Heart

Remember: little is much when God is in it. The words of this little hymn reveal the struggle and longing of the writer's soul to surrender to God's purposes. Ask God to give you one phrase from this hymn that will help open your eyes and ears to his steady presence and his echoes of mercy.

Spirit of God, descend upon my heart;
Wean it from earth, through all its pulses move;
Stoop to my weakness, mighty as thou art,
And make me love thee as I ought to love.

I ask no dream, no prophet ecstasies,
No sudden rending of the veil of clay,
No angel visitant, no op'ning skies;
But take the dimness of my soul away.

Hast thou not bid us love thee, God and King?
All, all thine own, soul, heart, and strength and
       mind.
I see thy cross—there teach my heart to cling:
O let me seek thee, and O let me find.

Teach me to feel that thou art always nigh;
Teach me the struggles of the soul to bear,

To check the rising doubt, the rebel sigh;
Teach me the patience of unanswered prayer.

Teach me to love thee as thine angels love,
One holy passion filling all my frame;
The baptism of the heav'n-descended Dove,
My heart an altar, and thy love the flame.

Other Hopeful Ideas

Do you believe that God will meet all your needs? Do not hesitate to verbalize your longing for God to restore your soul. He is pleased when we plead with him because we know he is the only One who can meet our deepest heart needs. Do not define for him what the restoration must be. I call such gems treasures in darkness. Some people call them God sightings or love notes from God.

Whatever you call them, after pleading with him for mercy, recognize when he sends the evidences of his presence and allow him to love you *his* way. The most reliable messages we receive are from his Word. In Deuteronomy 6:6–7 God commanded the Israelites to integrate his words into every aspect of their lives. His instructions have not changed. I interpreted God's promise to give me treasures in the darkness, riches stored in secret places as an exhortation to look for and expect them. What may have appeared to others as worthless drops of mercy, I learned to gratefully receive like a woman dying from thirst. Many mornings God started my day with echoes of his mercy in the writings of Oswald Chambers in *My Utmost for His Highest* and Mrs. Charles E. Cowman in *Streams in the Desert*. Both writers regularly challenged broken people like me to open our eyes to the tiny gems of God's love.

At first I was too weary to write out the specifics of how God spoke to me through such short devotional readings, but I wanted a record of God's intimate communication. In my journal I often noted on specific dates, "See *Streams*" or "See *Utmost*," and in the books I noted the year that God used the message of that entry.

Another way to intentionally confront yourself with his truth is to write out Scriptures (perhaps the ones listed in Scriptural Gems in this chapter) on 3 x 5 cards. Place them in strategic places throughout your home, car, and workplace.

Prayer: Open Their Eyes

O Lord, please help my dear sisters who are longing right at this very moment for a word from you. Open their spiritual eyes and ears to the riches stored in secret places, evidences of your constant presence. Amen.

8

WHO'S BEARING WHOSE BURDEN?

THE TREASURE OF ENCOURAGEMENT

 MIDNIGHT PRINCIPLE: God's people can help me bear burdens, but they cannot take them completely away.

JOURNAL INSIGHT

September 25, 1993, Sunday: Days after Mark's death Chuck told the children and me, "I am empty. But I promise you that on Sundays you will hear what God is saying to me in my own struggles. The only help I can give you right now is my preaching."

Today on this your day, I anticipated hearing from you, Lord. I know that you are speaking through your Word as Chuck preaches, because I see his condition on Saturday nights. He is weak, wants to run away, hopeless, the task of preaching is beyond his ability. The supernatural transformation that happens between Saturday night and Sunday morning confronts me with the reality of you. Only you could change the broken, shattered, doubting man from Saturday night into this giant of faith that I hear preach with honesty and power on Sunday mornings. He is not pretending faith. He reminds me of the psalmists who start out with cries of despair and questions and end with settled faith.

For the past two weeks he has preached on the theme When God Doesn't Make Sense. He read James Dobson's book with the same title while we were at the family reunion. Chuck told the congregation that it's the only book that has helped him so far. The title drew him in, and he hoped to find resolution for some of his questions. He concluded with the author that some times God doesn't make sense; that's why we must walk by faith, trusting him to be perfect in love and mercy.

His messages are reminding me: True healing begins with right doctrine. If your doctrine doesn't work in the funeral home, it's worthless. Be sure that what you believe is what the

Scripture teaches; When Satan whispers lies in one ear, choose to hear God whispering truth in the other; When we know God is sovereign, there are no "if onlys."

He closed with the words, "Like a mighty python, fear encircles you whenever you experience sudden extended pain. The strangling circle of fear is so intense that it demands faithful friends who will empathize with the sudden loss and not avoid it. The Body has incredible power to heal one of its members. We have the foundation of Christ and we need the Body of Christ to believe for us when we can't believe for ourselves (Ex. 17:11–12). When Moses could not physically do what God commanded, Aaron and Hur held up his hands for him.

"The circle of fear narrows as trustworthy friends direct us to the promises of God (Ex. 17:14). The strangling python of terror must loosen its grip as God's past faithfulness to others strengthens us in our journey (Ex. 17:15–16)."

Then Chuck paused before he challenged the congregation: "Are you willing to enter into the suffering of another and stay there with them until they experience the joy of the Lord?"

HELP ME!

Prior to Mark's death, I had the privilege of teaching about biblical encouragement. I had no idea our family's spiritual health and emotional healing would be so intimately intertwined with the principles I taught the women of our church. Four months after losing Mark, I spoke at a women's conference and described the many practical ways our church family had encouraged us in this journey through grief. I closed my remarks with these words:

> I am a woman in process. I am choosing to believe the promises of God. Oswald Chambers said, "If through a broken heart God can bring His purposes to pass in the world, then thank Him for breaking your heart." My desire is that God will use my broken heart for his purposes. One day I hope that I will be able to go to a newly bereaved mother, perhaps one of you. I will cry with you. I will not judge you. No matter what comes out of your mouth. And I believe I will be able to offer you the hope and assurance that God is the healer of broken hearts, the restorer of broken walls, that he does bring beauty from ashes, and that he does make all things beautiful in his time. I believe I will be able to say these things in part, because the Body of Christ extended to me the heartfelt ministry of encouragement and became a physical demonstration of God's love. They entered into the chamber of sorrow and exhorted me to believe the promises of God. I beg you, listen to the nudge of the Holy Spirit. He wants you to experience the joy of being a channel of his compassion as you help turn hearts toward his Son, Jesus.[1]

God's people are often the vehicles through which he keeps his many promises. I don't know what I would have done without the cards, casseroles, caring attention of my congregation. But I know it's possible that this celebration of my church has left you feeling more alone and isolated than ever, because you have not experienced such care. I long for every person to experience God's love through the care of his or her local church. Unfortunately I understand the fear and ignorance of those who do not obey the encouragement mandate. Even now, when confronted with someone else's sorrow, I am sometimes afraid to step too close. In this chapter, we'll discuss some biblical and practical insights about our expectations of comfort from others.

The Issue of Expectations

"I hope I have some friends left by the time I get to the other side of this gulf of grief," I said to my sister. Spending time with me was not an easy task. And my friends did not have much more experience in this abyss of death than I did. Sometimes broken people change into strangers, and it scares those who love us. We struggle with conflicting emotions. Months into the journey, I told a trusted friend that I was depending on her to help me discern what was truth and what was a lie. My expectation of people—realistic or unrealistic—was a hard issue to sort out.

September 1993. I want to stay in bed, rolled up in a ball. Instead I choose to get up, prepare breakfast, start the wash, read my Bible, write in this journal. Tears are my constant companion. Chuck says I sigh constantly. So does he. I am irritable, edgy. Susan [Hunt] called. As soon as she asked, "How are you doing today?" angry words rolled up from somewhere deep inside. "Chuck is suffering so badly, and no one is reaching out to him. I'm so mad at the men who should be staying close. Why aren't pastors who know how lonely pain

in the ministry can be . . . where are they? I understand why
people get mad at the church when they are hurting. . . ."
Venomous words flowed like rolling lava. She remained silent
until the words stopped gushing. Her thoughtful response made
me angrier. "Sharon, we need to pray that God will reveal how
he wants you and Chuck to use this experience to teach the
church how to be encouragers when crisis hits." I stopped her
and spit out, "Susan, you pray about it. I don't care about the
church. We have nothing to offer anyone. I just want someone to help my husband. How many of us have to have our
hearts broken before the church does what God already told
them to do? How many more books do they need? They won't
read them anyway!" Then I apologized to my friend who has
earned the right to confront my anger with truth.

She laughed and said, "You can beat on my chest any
time. And I am going to pray about how God will redeem this
pain for the good of his church."

After we hung up, I thought about our conversation.
What did I really want? Someone to fix my husband—to give
him whatever he needs to be my protector, the one who has
always led me into your truth. I want my husband back. But
no one can fix him or me. No one can take away our longing
for what was. Perhaps my expectations are unfair. But if a man
asked me what he could do for Chuck, I would tell him,

"Don't assume that because he's the pastor he's strong. Don't let his grief intimidate you. He needs friends who are not afraid to ask the hard questions and will not run from his pain. Ask him, 'How can I pray for you today? How did your day go, really? What was good? What was the worst part of your day? Let's meet for lunch. How about a round of golf? Talk to me. What are your hardest times of the day? I want to pray specifically at those times.'" And then be willing to spend time with a once-strong man who is broken with grief and sometimes a stranger.

This is a moment where I must stop my emotions from telling me lies. There are men who have done those things and I'm grateful. People are helping us, they are trying to carry the load with us. But they can't fix us.

Susan's words confronted me with what I already know. You will not waste this experience. You want us to offer it back to you for you to use to build your church. Thinking rightly about this is exhausting, but Susan is reminding me of good theology. I have a responsibility to one day allow you to redeem this pain in a way that will equip others to walk in the darkness with broken-hearted people. I don't want to think about that right now. I'm just too tired. Chuck says we are like two wounded soldiers trying to help each other off the battle-field while the guns are blazing and bombs are exploding all *around us. I picture us as two confused, vacant-eyed, terrified lost souls wandering through a deep, dark forest packed with things that go "boo!" at midnight. We hear each other's fear-filled voices, calling for help, but we can't get through the tight brush and trees. Sometimes our fingertips touch and we hope for a tighter clasp, but the monsters of despair and hopelessness yank us apart and we are alone once more. But are we alone?*

This journal entry reflects the frustration many hurting people express over the seeming neglect of the church when it comes to encouragement. Our church did not neglect us, but my desperate longing for resolution of my pain became fertile ground for hurt to root.

God answered Susan's prayer by leading me to write a book on the ministry of encouragement, *Treasures of Encouragement*.[2] Through my study for that book, I realized how simple biblical encouragement really is. The most effective encouragers for me were those who understood that their role was not to make me better. Their job was to consider carefully how their actions could help turn my heart toward the only One who could make me better. Their prayerful merciful acts transformed them into "God with skin on."

THE PURPOSE OF BIBLICAL ENCOURAGEMENT

The purpose of biblical encouragement is to turn our hearts toward God. Perhaps I was so frustrated and angry about the men I perceived to be neglecting my husband because I had a skewed definition of encouragement. I wanted someone to fix Chuck.

Seeing his raw grief and not being able to help him tore out my heart. I had lost not only my son but also the security of my husband. Chuck was my rock, the one who could fix anything. Who would fix me now? And who would fix him?

Often people don't extend themselves to help broken people because they know they can't fix them. What could they do for us? They couldn't bring back Mark.

At some point, my cry changed from "give me my son or I will die" to "give me yourself, God, or I will die." In *Treasures of Encouragement* I describe how God guided that transition:

> In the months following Mark's death, I rushed home from every errand, eagerly sorted mail, and anxiously listened to phone messages. When I asked myself, "Why are you so desperate for mail and phone calls?" I realized I was hoping someone—anyone—would relieve the unending ache in my heart. When the phone did not ring, cards did not come, and no one visited, my shattered heart begged for physical comfort.
>
> On those days God helped me realize that He alone was my encourager. All of the encouragement I had received from the body were initiated by Him and came from Him. I knew, therefore, that He was sufficient even on the days when I had no physical evidence of God's presence.
>
> The phone calls, cards, and visits were pinpoints of relief, but I still had to face the emptiness of each day without my youngest child. God knew that the resolution for me would be to embrace the truth of the message one friend sent: "There are some wounds only heaven can heal."
>
> Through excruciating confusion and grief, I learned that the purpose of all encouragement is to point us to the satisfaction only God can give.[3]

THE TREASURE OF ENCOURAGEMENT

> May the LORD answer you when you are in distress: may
> the name of the God of Jacob protect you. May he send
> you help from the sanctuary and grant you support from
> Zion. (Ps. 20:1–2)

If ever our local church looked like our sanctuary or the beautiful Bride of Christ, it was in the months following Mark's death. The actions of our congregation demonstrated that we were not alone in our sorrow.[4]

This is not to say that everyone said and did exactly what we needed. We have our list of hurtful moments when the wrong words or actions seemed to make our sorrow deeper. After such an incident, a friend challenged me, "Try to remember 'intent' versus 'impact.' Give people the benefit of the doubt and don't get stuck in anger or bitterness."

God created us to need each other and often keeps his promises of comfort and strength through other believers. God repeatedly reminds us to encourage one another. The challenge of Paul in Galatians 6:2, "Bear ye one another's burdens, and so fulfil the law of Christ" (KJV), teaches us that God expects us to not only need each other but also to reflect the love of Christ by helping each other. Grief is not a pathway we should attempt to walk alone. Friends of ours who did not find that help through their church found it in a grief support group. The other members of the group understood their unique relationship to their child and patiently listened as they tried to articulate their longing for what was. Then gently reminded them that "there is a time to heal, to weep, to mourn." And then they helped them understand how to laugh and dance again (Eccl. 3:3–4).

God can also use written and multimedia resources as channels of his compassion when our network is busy with other responsibilities.

Sometimes we get so focused on our need for others that we demand they carry our burdens. We forget the rest of the passage in Galatians 6:5 that commands each of us to "carry our own burdens." Our goal must always be to one day be the comforter, the one who encourages the brokenhearted that they can trust God, even in their present darkness.

But at the end of the day, it's the encouragement of God that sustains us and brings beauty from the ashes of our burned-up dreams. Next to 1 Peter 5:7, "Cast all your cares on him, for he careth for you" I have noted the date, November 16, 1994, and wrote, "In a note from a friend to Daniel. God's still small voice to me." Next to Galatians 5:10 I wrote a date with the words, "Roberta called." Seeing that notation reminded me of the pity party I was having and God's response through this phone call: "And the God of all grace, who called you to his eternal glory in Christ, after you have suffered a little while, will himself restore you and make you strong, firm and steadfast."

I now see that this threefold partnership—others, self, God—was evident in a journal entry, based on an October sermon outline.

October 1993. In his Sunday message Chuck gave us some practical steps for facing temptation and depression. I tried to take those steps today.

1. Thank God for this opportunity to learn more about trusting him. I'm afraid that the words of thanks stick in my throat. But I am choosing to say them anyway.

2. Quote a Scripture verse that addresses the need of the moment. Today mine is Ephesians 2:10: "For we are God's workmanship, created in Christ Jesus to do good works, which

God prepared in advance for us to do." God has clearly called me to the tasks of this day. Therefore, he has equipped me to perform them. I am choosing to believe that promise though my emotions beg to differ.

3. Call a friend for prayer. I called Diane and told her I felt as though demons inhabit our house, hiding behind the furniture, waiting to jump out and terrify me. . . . demons of doubt, fear, longing for what was. No matter what I did, I couldn't stop crying. She immediately prayed for relief and protection.

4. Move. If I am lying down, sit up. If I am sitting, stand up. If I am standing, start walking. If I am walking, start running. Today I chose with my will to weed the front flowerbeds. About half way through the job, I picked up the hand spade and repeatedly slammed it into the ground, tears streaming down my cheeks, wanting to scream and scream. Chuck told us that if the steps aren't working to start over again. I didn't have the strength to start over again, to thank you for this opportunity to grow. Instead, I wanted to lie in the dirt and give in to the tears. Just then Chuck walked up behind me, gently touched my shoulder before handing me a pink envelope. Inside was a message written by the hand of my friend, Carolyn, clearly a special delivery love note from my heavenly Father: "God Himself has said, I will not in any

way fail you nor give you up nor leave you without support. [I will] not, [I will] not, [I will] not in any degree leave you helpless nor forsake you nor let [you] down (relax My hold on you). [Assuredly not!] (Heb. 13:5, AMP).

For reasons I did not understand at the time, these words broke the physical ache in my chest and relieved the soul pain for a few hours. I felt hugged by my heavenly Father, and the tears that streamed were cleansing. I felt almost normal and was able to prepare dinner and complete other daily tasks with a grateful heart.

My burden bearers indeed carried the burden of the day. But on the days they didn't, I tried to remember that God alone is the source of all encouragement. Whatever he had given me for that day was all I needed.

TREASURES OF HOPE

Scriptural Gems

"Why are you downcast, O my soul? Why so disturbed within me? Put your hope in God, for I will yet praise him, my Savior and my God." (Ps. 42:5)

"Show me your ways, O LORD, teach me your paths; guide me in your truth and teach me, for you are God my Savior, and my hope is in you all day long." (Ps. 25:4–5)

"Two are better than one, because they have a good return for their work. If one falls down, his friend can help him up. But pity the man who falls and has no one to help him up! Also if two lie down together, they will keep warm. But how can one keep warm alone? Though one may be overpowered, two can defend themselves. A cord of three strands is not quickly broken." (Eccl. 4:9–12)

Songs in the Night: Be Still, My Soul

September 8, 1993. Dear Father, I'm in Mark's room, converted into an office. The odor of fresh paint obliterates the scent of beat-up, stinky sneakers, dirty clothes, and Mark's cologne. I am alone. I give myself permission to grieve without restraint. To try to make sense of a senseless world.

As I close my Bible, you open my ears to the music playing in the background, the sweet, soothing hymn "Be Still, My Soul." I hear your voice, Father. You are rocking your weeping, exhausted daughter. You whisper in my ears. You hate death. But fresh grief is deaf, and I didn't want to hear anything from you. . . . I am confused. But I am beginning to see your love drawing me, in spite of myself. Your people surround me with love in the midst of their own grief. Their actions help me see you. And I hear you. For now, for this moment, I hear you: "My precious daughter, my brokenhearted child. Be still and know that I am God." Lord, help me, help me to be still.

Sometimes we need to actually exhort our souls to walk by faith against our emotions and logic. This hymn by Katharina Van Schlegel seems to do just that and resonates with the prayers of the psalmist when he talks to himself in Psalm 42:5: "Why are you downcast, O my soul? Why so disturbed within me? Put your hope in God, for I will yet praise him, my Savior and my God."

Especially note the last verse that so beautifully reminds us of the day when all tears will be wiped away and death will be no more.

Be still, my soul: the Lord is on your side;
Bear patiently the cross of grief or pain;
Leave to your God to order and provide;
In ev'ry change he faithful will remain.
Be still, my soul: your best, your heav'nly Friend
Through thorny ways lead to a joyful end.

Be still, my soul: your God will undertake
To guide the future as he has the past.
Your hope, your confidence let nothing shake;
All now mysterious shall be bright at last.
Be still, my soul: the waves and winds still know
His voice who ruled them while he dwelt below.

Be still, my soul: when dearest friends depart,
And all is darkened in the vale of tears,
Then shall you better know his love, his heart,
Who comes to soothe your sorrow and your fears.
Be still, my soul; your Jesus can repay
From his own fullness all he takes away.

Be still my soul: the hour is hast'ning on
When we shall be forever with the Lord,
When disappointment, grief, and fear are gone,
Sorrow forgot, love's purest joys restored.
Be still, my soul: when change and tears are past,
All safe and blessed we shall meet at last.

Other Hopeful Ideas

Have you been hurt by what you perceive as neglect by people you thought would never let you down? Has a good friend forgotten an important anniversary, birthday, or to return a call? Did she take too long to contact you after your loss, or did she neglect to send a card at all? When she came to comfort you, did she talk about her own problems, insignificant in the face of your darkness? Is anger smoldering in your heart toward a once-loved companion?

Every morning when you wake up, think, God has given me just enough energy for the grief work of this day. I must choose carefully how I will spend it. Do I have enough to invest in anger toward a friend who has neglected to encourage me? Is it possible for me to use my limited energy to think of one thing for which I can thank God?

Describe your hurt to God. Cry out to him that even those you depended on have forsaken you. Ask God for strength to love those who have disappointed you. You have a choice: hold on to bitterness toward those who disappoint you or forgive them or learn to forgive them for their ignorance. With a choice of your will, acknowledge that your only hope is in him. Personalize, pray, and journal with the Scriptures listed above.

Start a Treasures of Encouragement record in your journal. Write across the top of a page in your journal, "I thank my God every time I remember . . ." (Phil. 1:3). Begin listing the treasures God has sent your way to turn your heart toward him. Especially thank God for specific messages of hope you have received through others, whether in the flesh or through books, radio programs, a song, pamphlets, videos, and taped messages.

If you have children, use this exercise to encourage them to open up about their feelings—and in this way be an encouragement to them. Gather construction paper, glitter, stickers, crayons, magic markers, and scissors. Prepare a simple snack. Write out these Scriptures or other favorite verses on 3 x 5 cards and glue them on construction paper. Explain to your child that you want him or her to help you make posters that you will place throughout your house to help you remember to think what God thinks. Read the verses together. As you are working draw out the child by asking questions like:

What do you think this verse means?

Jesus says he is the Good Shepherd and lays down his life for his sheep. How does that help you trust him to be close to you when you are afraid?

I get scared sometimes, do you?

What makes you afraid?

What's your favorite memory?

What's your saddest memory?

As you talk, share what Scripture phrases mean the most to you and underline or frame them in a bold way. Explain how important it is to choose to believe what God says when your emotions take you somewhere else.

Prayer: Teach Us

O Father, teach us how to allow the treasures of encouragement from others to turn our hearts toward the hope and comfort we have in you. Show us where our expectations of human comfort are unrealistic and how to be still and rest in your strength. Amen.

9

$\mathcal{E}$VEN IN $\mathcal{E}$XILE, $\mathcal{C}$HOOSING $\mathcal{L}$IFE

THE TREASURE OF BUILDING A LEGACY

MIDNIGHT PRINCIPLE: Choosing life in the shadow of death helps create a spiritual legacy for generations to come.

JOURNAL INSIGHT

December 10, 1993. Heidi's wedding day! How precious our daughter is to me. No child could be more loved. When I was pregnant, Chuck and I would lie on the bed and wait patiently for her to start moving so that her daddy could feel her little body. After her birth, I tightly held her, reluctant to give her up to others. If I didn't hear her breathing at night, I touched her back, terrified she might have died in her sleep. All through her life she has seemed older than her years, sometimes like a little old lady in a child's body.

I have anticipated her wedding day from the time I first counted her toes and fingers. We prayed for her future husband, trusting you to bring just the right man into her life. So we already love Greg because we covered him with prayer before we knew him. He is getting a wife who is more precious than fine rubies.

O Father, protect them and give them the desire of their hearts, that their marriage reflect you and your relationship to the church. Give them joy, joy that only you can give.

LIFE IN THE MIDST OF DEATH

A New Level of Normal

One of the most freeing pieces of advice for us was when a friend said, "Don't let anyone tell you that it's time to get back to normal. You will never be normal again, but that's not necessarily a bad thing. You must find a new level of normal in which to live your daily life."

The major thread in the fabric of our lives was the death of our son. "New normal" for us meant allowing God to transform what looked like a bloody, frayed rope into a strand of gold that glowed with his power and strength.

In the months following Mark's death I had only so much energy for each day, and a good friend challenged me that the labor before me was grief work. I was exhausted, and every joint ached. Groups of chattering people wearied me, and I couldn't think straight or easily make decisions. I often joked that when Mark went to heaven, he took my memory with him. But it wasn't really a joke. I intentionally scaled back other responsibilities in order to lean into the pain and learn how to make it my friend and counselor.

Sometimes I felt guilty because I had stepped out of women's ministry and other responsibilities to focus on the hard work of grief. At those moments I reminded myself that I was seeking a new normal. God affirmed my decision with Jesus' instructions to his disciples during one of his postresurrection appearances: "Do not leave Jerusalem, but wait for the gift my Father promised, which you have heard me speak about" (Acts 1:4b).

From this encounter I trusted him to let me know when it was time to step back into active ministry. For now I needed the balm of his love to soothe and heal before I could meet the needs of anyone outside of my family. But I could not be self-centered in my grief. Healing required touching the lives of others. My new normal meant that whatever energy I had would go into grief work and trying to minister to my husband and children.

Wedding Plans

The wedding plans of our only daughter and oldest son confronted us with a dilemma. Heidi and Greg had planned to be married in December, six months after Mark's death. Young Chuck planned to marry Melanie the next summer. How could we rejoice when anguish shadowed every breath? Mark's death shredded the hearts of his older sister and two brothers. Each one responded differently. Heidi ran to Greg, her fiancé, and deepened her commitment to him. By contrast, the loss of his brother opened young Chuck's soul to the possibility that life held more losses, and he couldn't imagine surviving any of them. So days after Mark's death he broke off his relationship with the person he loved more than anyone else, Melanie. He reasoned that if he didn't marry her, he wouldn't risk the heartbreak of losing her. Friends and family helped him see that living life in the context of fear was not God's way. He realized the poet's wisdom: "It's better to have loved and lost than never to have loved." Twenty-four hours after breaking up with her, Chuck asked Melanie to marry him. All the members of both families witnessed his proposal.

Throughout our only daughter's life, her dad and I looked forward to the fun of planning her wedding. As we tried to enter into the joyful anticipation of our daughter's special day, we realized that death creates an ever-widening circle of losses. What should have been months of laughter and fun were often covered with a shroud of sorrow. Before Mark's death I would have had no trouble with the many wedding decisions. Now decisions wearied me, and I had trouble thinking logically. Friends and family surrounded us with their help, but I should have been more involved. The day Heidi gently prodded, "Mom, I want you to do one thing this week: Pick out a dress to wear for the wedding," I recognized how little help I was to her and for her. I tried to give my regret to God and intentionally moved deeper into the plans.

An Elephant in the Room

A few years after Heidi's wedding, I expressed regret that sorrow shadowed her special day. She stopped me and said, "Mom, my wedding day was exactly what I dreamed of and what I wanted, except for Mark's absence. So please don't ever feel like I was shortchanged."

Someone had given us a poem titled "An Elephant in the Room." It describes a young girl's frustration that her sister's death was like having a big elephant in the midst of a family event. Everyone pretended the elephant wasn't there. The bereaved author ends her poem with a plea that someone would say her sister's name so the girl could talk about her without fear. That poem helped articulate how we would consciously choose to face daily life, including landmark events like weddings. We acknowledged the "elephant in the room" while obeying God's command to "choose life": "This day I call heaven and earth as witnesses against you that I have set before you life and death, blessings and curses. Now choose life, so that you and your children may live and that you may love the LORD your God, listen to his voice, and hold fast to him. For the LORD is your life, and he will give you many years in the land he swore to give to your fathers, Abraham, Isaac and Jacob" (Deut. 30:19–20). At first this Scripture seemed like a slap. Was my child gone from this earth because I had not chosen life? I began to understand that this Scripture promises an eternal legacy to those who choose to trust God through his Son, Jesus. We needed to choose life in the context of that trust as a way to build a legacy of trusting God into our children and one day, their children.

Choose Life

I want to let Heidi describe her wedding—giving you the insight of a bride, carrying both joy and grief.

Like most girls, I had dreamed about my wedding all of my life. Even before July, Mom and I had found the perfect dress—hanging upstairs in my closet.

Three days after Mark died, I stood in the kitchen, surrounded by people. Someone asked me about the upcoming wedding. I fell apart. My mother immediately appeared, placed her hands on my arms, and firmly stated, "Your father and I believe you and Greg are ready for marriage. Your wedding and all the trimmings will go on as planned." I cried and said that we could wait a while. "We couldn't do it without Mark. How could we celebrate?" But Mom wouldn't let it go. My parents chose life for their daughter in the midst of death. This was the way it was going to be, end of discussion.

Planning a large wedding is difficult. Planning one in the context of sorrow is hard to describe. Over the next six months, I often used the word *funeral* when I meant to say "wedding." I had trouble making decisions; I wonder if I inadvertently hurt people with my foggy thinking. My family and friends stepped in and helped in amazing ways. Aunts selected and arranged all the flowers. Friends made Christmas-tree centerpieces. I even had help addressing invitations. Every weekend our closest friends became a circle of comfort and laughter for us and our parents as they spent time at our home. They encouraged me to talk and cry and dream . . . *new* dreams. Everything felt wrong, and yet marrying Greg felt so right.

As the days drew closer, I determined that Mark was not going to be the "elephant in the room." We did not replace him in the wedding party but instead left his spot empty. One of the bridesmaids walked alone. I wrote a letter to my family about Mark and the special memory I had of him seeing me in my wedding gown when I brought it home. My uncle graciously read the letter at our ceremony. We dedicated a special song to Mark and to my family, and encouraged them to be strong in God's love.

At the reception, our video included pictures of Mark. Taking family portraits without Mark was painful, but we acknowledged how hard it was by trying to joke as the cameras clicked. Whenever pain overwhelmed one of us, we didn't encourage each other to stop crying and be strong. Instead, we took a moment to cry and then stepped into the joy of the event. We hit it head on and didn't try to pretend that Mark was there in body. During our wedding dance, I caught a glimpse of my brother Chuck. He was in my grandmother's arms, sobbing. My wedding day was one of the hardest in that first year without Mark but also a reminder that God wanted us to live life joyfully in the context of eternity.

Heidi Needed Our Presence

Heidi's wedding day was beautiful but laced with sorrow. After checking on her progress getting dressed, I headed toward the sanctuary, when grief suddenly grabbed me. I stopped on the steps for a few seconds, took a deep breath, and prayed that God would transform the tears into strength for our family just for that moment. I closed my eyes, shook my head to clear it of sorrow, and continued on my way to the next task. Mark was physically gone, but Heidi was still here and needed her mother to step up to the plate on this day of days.

Chuck not only walked Heidi down the aisle but also performed the ceremony. My pastor brother was in the front pew ready to step in if Chuck could not carry on. Chuck did not want this night to be about him and his grief, so he prerecorded his message the night before. Through a prearranged sign, Chuck signaled the sound man to play the tape when he realized he could not speak the words he wanted Heidi and Greg to hear. Late that night we laughed and reminisced with good friends who helped us load up our car with wedding gifts. We were learning that to choose life would be hard, but the results were worth the effort.

THE TREASURE OF BUILDING A LEGACY

> Since my youth, O God, you have taught me, and to this
> day I declare your marvelous deeds. Even when I am old
> and gray, do not forsake me, O God, till I declare your
> power to the next generation, your might to all who are
> to come. (Ps. 71:17–18)

As a girl I memorized the answer to the Westminster Catechism question: "What is the chief end of man? The chief end
of man is to glorify God and to enjoy him forever." Mark's death
forced me to reconsider the meaning of those words. What does
that look like when all I can think about is what will never be—
the lost dreams and shattered plans?

In response to my search for eternal purpose, God gave me
some specific answers in Jeremiah 29. I was drawn to this chapter because of Jeremiah 29:11: " 'For I know the plans I have for
you,' declares the LORD, 'plans to prosper you and not to harm
you, plans to give you hope and a future.' "

How could this possibly apply to me? What a promise and so
simple to believe if the sun always shines on your daily life! But
this Scripture feels like salt in the wounds for suffering believers.
Is this Scripture only for people with enough faith? I suggest that
this passage is for every child of God whose circumstances are
painful, difficult. Not only is it overflowing with hope for brokenhearted people, but studying this verse in its context gives me
specific instructions for facing my future.

In Jeremiah 29 I see that these Israelites were my sisters and
brothers, longing for what had been. They were in captivity, in
Babylon, because of the sin of their nation, Judah. God took full
responsibility for this discipline. It would end in seventy years;
nothing they did would change the release date. The fact that
not even their enemies had the power to keep them trapped

beyond that time was one more reason for hope: God, not their captors, was in control of their destiny. And God always wraps grace around discipline. This was not a time to walk with bowed heads and hopeless hearts. This was a pathway that would bear great blessing if they could see their journey as God's perfect plan.

I imagine there were faithful Israelites whose hearts had never turned against their God. They were in captivity because of the sins of their countrymen. These faithful people had a choice, to grow in bitterness and cry out, "This isn't fair!" They could hate those who had caused their captivity. Or they could accept it as an opportunity to experience God's strength.

The writings of Francis Schaeffer, especially *Letters to My Students*, helped Chuck and me better understand that on some level we all live in exile, meaning we live in a sin-broken world. His conclusions helped me to better understand my circumstances. Identifying my "location" as broken took some of the shock and sting out of suffering. Of course, I will suffer in this world—it's broken!

God's "exile living instructions" to the Israelites captured my imagination. They are so practical, and I searched to understand how they applied to me.

> This is what the LORD Almighty, the God of Israel, says to all those I carried into exile from Jerusalem to Babylon: "Build houses and settle down; plant gardens and eat what they produce. Marry and have sons and daughters; find wives for your sons and give your daughters in marriage, so that they too may have sons and daughters. Increase in number there; do not decrease.
>
> "Also, seek the peace and prosperity of the city to which I have carried you into exile. Pray to the LORD for it, because if it prospers, you too will prosper." Yes, this

is what the LORD Almighty, the God of Israel, says: "Do not let the prophets and diviners among you deceive you. Do not listen to the dreams you encourage them to have. They are prophesying lies to you in my name. I have not sent them," declares the LORD. (Jer. 29:4–9)

Marrying, bearing children, building homes, planting gardens, growing families—all of these imply hope, not despair.

This was a challenging exhortation for the children of Israel, as it is for any child of God whose circumstances imprison her. Strangely, I gained hope when I calculated that the older generation hearing Jeremiah's words would not experience physical deliverance from their exile. The elderly Israelites would die in exile; others would grow old in captivity. Yet the promise of Jeremiah 29:11—God having a plan for them, giving them a hope and a future—still applied to them. God was telling them that their physical bondage would not end on this earth. His words and their circumstances confronted them with a choice: Grow in bitterness toward God or see the bigger, eternal picture. To make the second choice required that they surrender to the fact that their legacy for the next generation was more important than their personal freedom. Could they choose God's enabling power to look past their own plight? Could they accept that their plight was a platform designed by God for the purpose of glorifying him? What a responsibility wrapped in privilege! Their response to these circumstances could help equip their families for their future pathways.

On some days, when grief threatened to undo me, my strength for the moment seemed to come as I thought of my responsibility to the younger generation, my children, their friends, and more recently my grandchildren. A key motivation for me to obey God when my emotions question his power is knowing that my journey might influence our children and grandchildren to trust him when the lights go out in their lives. Hard times will come. On what will the next generations of our family depend to help them more than survive in this broken world? Chuck and I challenge each other to remember that we need to live in such a way that generations coming after us will conclude that they can also trust God. Mere words would not cut it. We had to let them witness our experience of his presence.

TREASURES OF HOPE

Scriptural Gems

"But if serving the LORD seems undesirable to you, then choose for yourselves this day whom you will serve, whether the gods your forefathers served beyond the River, or the gods of the Amorites, in whose land you are living. But as for me and my household, we will serve the LORD." (Josh. 24:15)

"We will tell the next generation the praiseworthy deeds of the LORD, his power, and the wonders he has done . . . so the next generation would know them, even the children yet to be born, and they in turn would tell their children. Then they would put their trust in God and would not forget his deeds but would keep his commands." (Ps. 78:4, 6–7)

"Great is the LORD and most worthy of praise; his greatness no one can fathom. One generation will commend your works to another; they will tell of your mighty acts. They will speak of the glorious splendor of your majesty, and I will meditate on your wonderful works. They will tell of the power of your awesome works. . . . They will tell of the glory of your kingdom and speak of your might, so that all men may know of your mighty acts and the glorious splendor of your kingdom. Your kingdom is an ever-lasting kingdom, and your dominion endures through all generations. The LORD is faithful to all his promises and loving toward all he has made." (Ps. 145:3–6, 11–13)

"How can we sing the songs of the LORD while in a foreign land? If I forget you, O Jerusalem, may my right hand forget its skill." (Ps. 137:4–5)

Songs in the Night: Shine, Jesus Shine

One of the last things Mark did on this earth was practice playing his new drum set with his band in preparation for an upcoming youth concert. The year before Mark had asked his dad for permission to play his drums as part of the worship team in our church. Chuck had responded, "We don't use drums in the church. No." Mark challenged him, "Dad, if I can't play my drums for the Lord in the church, where can I play them?"

Mark's question challenged Chuck to think carefully about the exhortation of Scripture that we must give all of our gifts and talents to our Lord for the purpose of kingdom building. He gave young Chuck permission to put together a worship team, using guitars and drums. Our leaders decided that our worship should be a blend of the great hymns and contemporary music. Mark's genuine question to his dad helped shape the music legacy of our church. "Shine, Jesus, Shine" soon became one of the most loved contemporary songs for our congregation. We sang it at Mark's coronation service. Carefully read the words and recognize that the ultimate purpose of basking in the light of Christ is to become a light in the darkness for the generations to come.

> Lord, the light of your love is shining
> In the midst of the darkness shining.
> Jesus, Light of the world, shine upon us.
> Set us free by the truth you now bring us.
> Shine on me, shine on me.

[Refrain]
Shine, Jesus, shine,
Fill this land with the Father's glory,
Blaze, Spirit, blaze,
Set our hearts on fire.
Flow, river, flow,
Flood the nations with grace and mercy,
Send forth your Word, Lord,
And let there be light.

Lord, I come to your awesome presence
From the shadows into your radiance.
By the blood I may enter your brightness,
Search me, try me, consume all my darkness.
Shine on me, shine on me.

As we gaze on your kingly brightness,
So our faces display your likeness;
Ever changing from glory to glory,
Mirrored here, may our lives tell your story.
Shine on me, shine on me.[1]

Other Hopeful Ideas

You may not have children. You may be facing life alone.
But God's Word still is full of hope and specific instructions just
for you. Read through Jeremiah 29. In your journal, list God's
instructions for living in a broken world:

Build houses and settle down.
Plant gardens and eat what they produce.
Marry and have sons and daughters.
Find wives for your sons and give your daughters in mar-
     riage so that they too may have sons and daughters.

Increase in number there. Do not decrease.
Seek the peace and prosperity of the city to which I have
carried you into exile.
Pray to the Lord for it, because if it prospers, you too will
prosper.
Live in the context of my truth, not the lies of false
prophets.

If you are fresh in your grief, this list will overwhelm you, but ask
God to start planting hope in your heart as you slowly consider
how you can live out these instructions in your broken world.

Is it time to take back responsibility for caring for your home?

Is it time to reach out and help another person? (Planting a
garden may not mean a literal garden but rather starting to reach
out to meet small needs in another person's life.)

How does God's instruction to marry and have sons and daughters apply to you? I see this as an exhortation to invest in my marriage and remaining children even though my emotional resources
are almost nonexistent. The stress of grief reveals the cracks in a
marriage. Is it time to address those cracks with God's love?

How does this apply if you are single or childless? This leads
into God's direction to "seek the peace and prosperity" of the
place you are in; let's say that's the "city" of your grief. "Pray to
the Lord for it, because if it prospers, you too will prosper." In
other words, be intentional about seeing your circle of influence
as an opportunity to reflect the presence of God—an opportunity
to choose life. Your cooperation with God's purposes will eventually reap peace for you and build into others a legacy of grace
and strength.

Prayer: Tell the Next Generation

Father, through blurry eyes we read your instructions; they
are more than some of us can bear or understand. Sometimes

you seem to be a hard taskmaster, yet you created us and know what will make us whole once more. You are patient and know that we are frail. O God, show us how to trust and obey your exhortation to tell the next generation of your goodness, so that they will trust you, too.

10

THE SPIRIT OF CHRISTMAS PRESENT

THE TREASURE OF HOLIDAY PRESENCE

MIDNIGHT PRINCIPLE: The Christmas story itself can give strength through the holiday season.

JOURNAL INSIGHT

Sunday, December 19, 1993. Chuck's message gives me permission to step back from the glitz of Christmas without guilt. For some reason it helps me to know that the coming of Messiah was a time of pain and weeping. Jesus did not come as a conquering king but a suffering servant. The shepherds were watching over temple sheep that were set apart for slaughter as sacrifices. God chose for Jesus to be born into the rule of a cruel, brutal man. Herod had killed every member of his family that he suspected of disloyalty. The arrival of the wise men from Iran and Iraq terrified Herod. He was so frightened by their search for the baby who would be king that he ordered every baby boy under the age of two to be killed.

Matthew 2:17–18: "Then what was said through the prophet Jeremiah was fulfilled: 'A voice is heard in Ramah, weeping and great mourning, Rachel weeping for her children and refusing to be comforted, because they are no more.'" This terrible loss was prophesied in Jeremiah 31:15. O God, you knew. You knew. Somehow that comforts me. There are no accidents.

Mary, the mother of Jesus, is told that a sword will pierce her soul as a result of the birth and life of this child. O God, what did Christmas really cost?

IN THE BLEAK MIDWINTER

Isaiah's Sustenance

Holidays sharpen grief. Celebrating such a treasured family holiday was on our minds even on that terrible July night when we lost Mark. On our way home from the hospital, Chuck grabbed my hand and barely whispered, "Christmas, how can we ever celebrate Christmas?"

I had no answer.

Christmas had always been my favorite time of year. We didn't buy many toys for our children throughout the year; that was reserved for Christmas. What great fun we always had, planning and preparing, watching for sales, loving the adrenalin of the chase and the victory of finding just the right gift at just the right price. When Mark and Daniel had wanted the most popular toy, we had done everything we could to find it. We had perpetuated our childhood family traditions; family and friends always joined us for a Christmas Eve buffet and then attended the church communion service. I always loved the candlelight service, the music, the family feeling, the preaching, the security of old family traditions. Afterwards our immediate family had gathered at our home for the kids to exchange gifts and enjoy the euphoria of Christmas.

On the night of Mark's death, I concluded I would never experience such joy again.

After Heidi and Greg's wedding, I searched the Scriptures for direction on how to face this first Christmas as an incomplete family. Someone had told us that we should prepare for holidays, anniversaries, and birthdays by changing our traditions. The second half of the book of Isaiah seemed to affirm that suggestion, and I asked God for specific ways to help my family honor Christ's birth in the context of deep grief.

In my journal I wrote out passages from Isaiah as God's personal Christmas card to me and to remind me of his instructions. Some of those verses are here; some are in the Scriptural Gems section later in the chapter.

> But now, this is what the LORD says—he who created you, O Jacob, he who formed you, O Israel: "Fear not, for I have redeemed you; I have summoned you by name; you are mine. When you pass through the waters, I will be with you; and when you pass through the rivers, they will not sweep over you. When you walk through

the fire, you will not be burned; the flames will not set you ablaze." (Isa. 43:1–2)

"Forget the former things; do not dwell on the past. See, I am doing a new thing! Now it springs up; do you not perceive it? I am making a way in the desert and streams in the wasteland." (Isa. 43:18–19)

"Even to your old age and gray hairs I am he, I am he who will sustain you. I have made you and I will carry you; I will sustain you and I will rescue you." (Isa. 46:4)

"Then you will know that I am the LORD; those who hope in me will not be disappointed." (Isa. 49:23b)

Decoration-Day Meltdown

As the world around me laughed and anticipated a joyous Christmas filled with packages and food and family, I wished we could skip from Thanksgiving to the middle of January. I pleaded with God that he direct my steps through this quagmire of sorrow. I listened carefully as Chuck described the first Christmas as a season wrapped in pain, not fancy paper and bows. Blood and death covered that holy season. Eternal life could not come without such anguish.

December 20, 1993. I'm coming apart and I don't want to. The weekend went remarkably well. I felt almost strange. Mark seemed to be close by. After the wonderful choir cantata, Sean Delaney sheepishly pulled me aside and said, "I don't want to intrude on your family, but your sister told me to give you this. I'm not sure why, but I think it's a

Christmas gift from God for your family." He handed me a short manuscript, which I tucked into my bag as our family left for a local restaurant. We talked about Mark and laughed, teeter tottering between hysteria and calm.

The Christmas story and Chuck's message overwhelmed me with a new understanding of who you are and what you did at Christmas. I'm trying to focus on the choice Jesus made to be a suffering servant and that what he is asking of us is not more than he himself has done. But the ghost of grief is stalking me every minute, and I am weak in my own strength. I have so much I want to do for my family. I will not let the enemy use Mark's death to rob us of Christmas. But I don't know where to begin.

Psalm 86: Give me an undivided heart—where I will not be forever torn between missing Mark and trusting you. Deliver me from the pain of the grave. I have asked you to give me a sign of your goodness, that others will see your glory and come to you. I think Sean's story is one of those signs.

Christmas was on a Saturday that year. I was almost proud of the emotional control I had—focusing on Christ and the first Christmas—until Wednesday, when it was time to think about decorating the tree. I didn't think decorating would be a problem. But as I approached the attic, I started to cry. With each box I moved to get to the decorations, I cried harder. I found one of the boys' Star Wars men, and I cried. And then I found the decorations. On top was Mark's stocking. When I saw it, I laid my head down on the box and sobbed. Lord, why?

December 22. Chuck told me we don't need to do this—decorate. But I said, "Yes, we do. I want to recognize Christmas. We dishonor our son if we don't recognize his Savior's birth. We have to lean into the pain." Chuck pulled me down beside him on the sofa and said, "Then just sit here and cry for a while; don't try to hold it in." Finally, as he and young Chuck got the tree ready, I sorted through the decorations. I put most of them back. The stockings won't go up this year. Daniel put decorations on the tree with a smile, even when he found Mark's picture. This is all surreal. But we're getting through.

Safe Place of Comfort

December 23. We're following the advice of those who have walked this pathway before us, and we're changing our traditions. When friends realized I did not have the energy or desire to prepare a Christmas Eve buffet, they asked if they could prepare and serve all the food so that we could still gather together on such an important night. I am looking forward to being with the larger group tomorrow evening, but a dinner tonight will be my private gift to my family.

Lord, in answer to my plea to help me experience the joy of Christmas your way, you opened my eyes to treasures I can give to each one of my precious children and husband—the pictures, the story Sean wrote, the birthday letter Mark wrote to Chuck. You are leading me to use some traditions to create a safe place of comfort and to freely let go of other traditions without fear. Today I wept as I prepared all of Mark's favorite foods but smiled through tears as I remembered him coming in the back door, stretching his long arms to hang on the entry to the kitchen, and grinning with anticipation of eating hot Syrian bread, dripping with butter. I wished I could see him digging into the stuffed grape leaves one more time. Then I chose to imagine Mark at the banquet table in heaven with you. So, Lord, I'm preparing a special Christmas dinner with all of Mark's favorite foods, and we'll think of him enjoying the bounty of your grace while we enjoy the bounty of our Christmas table.

We had read that the anticipation of a holiday, anniversary, or birthday was often worse than the actual event, so one purpose of our family dinner was to create new traditions before Christmas day, hoping to ease in to the pain of Christmas. But my family didn't know that I had planned a few small surprises for each of them. After dinner Chuck asked the kids to join us in the family room in front of our glowing fireplace. I explained that our friend had written a story about our family and that I wanted to share it with them. We laughed and cried together as Sean's words poignantly and sometimes comically described our family experiencing the second coming of Christ during a future Christmas season. After the story I gave each of the kids framed pictures of Mark, each one captured a treasured memory with his siblings. I gave Chuck a plaque with the words, "Thanks, Dad, for always being there." And then I gave him the priceless gift of Mark's letter that I had found buried in my memories drawer.

Tears streamed down Chuck's cheeks as he read the framed words:

> Dad,
>
> In all the years that you have been my father there has not been a time when you failed to come through for me. There has not been a time when you failed to encourage me. You have always seen through me and my secretive ways and have not failed to counsel me when I need it most. The words "You're wrong and I'm right" are the words that I hate to hear the most but I thank you for them. You are a dad that many kids only dream of having, and I look up to you for all the knowledge that God has given you. I am proud to be called the "pastor's kid," because I believe it is worth dealing with all of the expectations that many people put on me. I thank God for you and the family he has given me each day. Any question that I ask you, you have never failed to answer it. Any problem that I bring to you, you never failed to help me through it. You have made sure that I am always happy and have never left me disappointed. Having you as my father is one of the best things God has given me. If I could repay you, I would, but I know that that is impossible. However, I can afford to tell you that I love you, and that I care about you very much.
>
> Love, Mark

December 24. Well, Lord, here I am. Christmas Eve. Running until I drop. Trying not to think. But I feel this might be the most important Christmas of my life. Mark's first Christmas in heaven. Our first Christmas without our child.

Changing Traditions

We felt loved by the friends who prepared and served the Christmas Eve buffet in our home before the communion service. In his Christmas Eve message Chuck shared with the congregation the Scriptures from Isaiah that were so comforting to us. By the time we sang "O Holy Night" at the end of the service, we were emotionally spent and drew strength from the hugs and tears of friends.

By Christmas morning we needed private family time. Instead of joining extended family for the traditional noisy celebration at the homes of our parents, we stayed at our house. Phone calls from family members meant so much as we tried to honor Christ and grieve for Mark at the same time.

THE TREASURE OF HOLIDAY PRESENCE

[Jesus said,] "I am with you always, to the very end of the age." (Matt. 28:20)

On Christmas day, I slipped away to spend time alone in our bedroom, reading the Christmas story, meditating especially on Mary and the conflicting emotions she must have experienced from the moment the angel told her about the coming Messiah. I wondered, *Was she lonely, afraid, confused? What emotions swirled around her soul when she gave birth to Jesus, far from family, disconnected from everything familiar?* I felt strangely drawn to her heart and the feelings she may have experienced on that dark, lonely night.

Mary's song, recorded in Luke 1:46–55, acknowledged her own need of a Savior and her absolute trust that God keeps his promises from generation to generation. I wondered if she sang this song as a sacrifice of praise, choosing to believe the promises of God in the context of unbelievable circumstances. I followed the thread of her story to the foot of the cross and wept as I married my longing for Mark to her anguish as she watched the brutalization of her beloved son. Did she wonder where God was? As if to answer my questions, God drew me back to the Scriptures from Isaiah where he repeatedly promised to never leave me alone, to guide me in the darkness, to never forget me, to always be with me. I remembered that Isaiah prophesied the virgin birth of Jesus and proclaimed that he would be called Immanuel, which means "God with us." The gospel of Matthew places this prophecy in the middle of the Christmas narrative (Matt. 1:23).

And do you know how Matthew ends his gospel? By his resurrection, Jesus has proven himself a victor over death. He's about to ascend to the right hand of his Father in heaven, and he promises his disciples—and his followers for generations to come—that he is not really leaving them. Jesus' last words: "Surely I am with you always, to the very end of the age."

Jesus, through his Spirit, is here. With us. With you. With me. Even now. Especially now, in the season that celebrates his birth.

TREASURES OF HOPE

Scriptural Gems
" 'I am the Lord's servant,' Mary answered. 'May it be to me as you have said.' " (Luke 1:38)

"Mary treasured up all these things and pondered them in her heart." (Luke 2:19)

What does Mary's song, the Magnificat, found in Luke 1:46–55, say to you about the character of God?

"Shout for joy, O heavens; rejoice, O earth; burst into song, O mountains. For the LORD comforts his people and will have compassion on his afflicted ones. But Zion said, 'The LORD has forsaken me; the LORD has forgotten me.' "Can a mother forget the baby at her breast and have no compassion on the child she has borne? Though she may forget, I will not forget you! See, I have engraved you on the palms of my hands; your walls are ever before me. Your sons hasten back, and those who laid you waste depart from you. Lift up your eyes and look around; all your sons gather and come to you, As surely as I live,' declares the LORD, 'you will wear them all as ornaments; you will put them on, like a bride.' " (Isa. 49:13–18)

Songs in the Night: O Holy Night

At first I didn't want to hear any Christmas carols, but then I began to listen carefully to the words. I grabbed on to the ones that proclaimed the "thrill of hope" that weary souls experienced with the entrance of the baby Jesus into a broken and shattered world. Take a few minutes and review "O Holy Night." Especially take notice of the second half of the second verse, "The King of kings lay thus in lowly manger, in all our trials born to be our Friend!"

Tell him your greatest need. Trust him to keep the promise of his presence, that he will never forsake his children. And trust that his presence is enough.

> O holy night, the stars are brightly shining;
> It is the night of the dear Savior's birth!

Long lay the world in sin and error pining,
Till he appeared and the soul felt its worth.
A thrill of hope, the weary soul rejoices,
For yonder breaks a new and glorious morn.
Fall on your knees, O hear the angel voices!
O night divine, O night when Christ was born!
O night, O holy night, O night divine!

Led by the light of faith serenely beaming,
With glowing hearts by his cradle we stand.
So led by light of a star sweetly gleaming,
Here came the wise men from Orient land.
The King of kings lay thus in lowly manger,
In all our trials born to be our Friend!
He knows our need—to our weakness is no stranger.
Behold your King; before him lowly bend!

Truly he taught us to love one another;
His law is love and his Gospel is peace.
Chains shall he break for the slave is our brother
And in his Name all oppression shall cease.
Sweet hymns of joy in grateful chorus raise we,
Let all within us praise his holy Name!
Christ is the Lord! O praise his name forever!
His pow'r and glory evermore proclaim!

Other Hopeful Ideas

Choosing to celebrate Christmas in the midst of deep grief requires leaning into the pain in order to strengthen broken places. Each family must decide the way that suits it best. I found it helpful to mix old traditions with new ones. Preparing Mark's favorite foods and planning small surprises for my family gave me a sense of joy. We gave ourselves permission to laugh and enjoy memories of Mark. Laughing did not mean we didn't miss Mark. We also gave ourselves permission to cry whenever and wherever we needed to cry.

I tried to take care of myself physically by continuing to walk regularly. For you it may be listening to music, shopping, playing sports, walking on the beach, or eating out with friends. Identify what comforts you and do it.

Friends commented that every time they heard "The Little Drummer Boy" they thought of Mark, our drummer. Collecting Little Drummer Boy memorabilia and drum tree ornaments became a quiet way to acknowledge Mark's continuing place in our family. What holiday memento collection might help you acknowledge your love for your departed family member?

Try to journal through the words of several Christmas carols, especially "O Little Town of Bethlehem." What "hopes and fears" do you have that can be met only in Christ?

Prayer: Hopes and Fears

Lord, the Christmas story tells us that your name is Immanuel, "God with us." Remind us that your Spirit is still with us. We give our hopes and fears to you, through this holiday and every day.

11

$\mathscr{S}$AFELY
$\mathscr{G}$ATHERED $\mathscr{I}$N

THE TREASURE OF A FATHER'S LOVE

> MIDNIGHT PRINCIPLE: As a child of God I am safely in his grip.

JOURNAL INSIGHT

April 23, 1994. Lord, I want to feel your arms around me, holding me, letting me cry, assuring me that everything will be all right. I need a Father whose presence brings strength and courage into the room.

Psalm 139:12 reminds me that you see darkness as an opportunity for your light to shine. Darkness is not to be dreaded by the child of God but seen as a precious time for knowing more deeply the love of the Father.

Father, you are using every means to remind me that you are close by, you know my doubts. It's as if you are holding me by the shoulders and saying, "Look at me. Look me in the eyes. Now, listen, hear me. I love you. You are my treasured possession (Deut. 7:6). Let me love you. Feel my arms around you. I am going to bring new life from this grave (Song 2:11–13). You can't see because you are afraid of the darkness and your eyes are scrunched shut against it. But I am the light (John 12:46). I am holding on to you (John 10:27–29). You will learn how to use this gift of grief to serve me, to glorify me (1 Peter 4:19). I will keep giving you the treasures of darkness. Open your eyes. See them. Don't define for me what those treasures must be. I am all-wise. I know what you need and I am giving it to you. Crawl up into my lap and let me love you. Let me love you my perfect way."

GOD'S GRAND LAP

The next day, after writing this entry, I received a note from a friend who urged me to curl up in God's lap.

And then a few days later at our grieving parents support group, one of the dads talked about his vision when he faced life-threatening surgery. All he could see was God's lap. He did not hear God's voice, but he saw himself crawl up into that grand lap, and there he felt a peace he had never before experienced.

The peace was so exquisite that he said he was willing to die if he could stay in God's lap. Of course he didn't die—he lived to tell the tale. Since that vision, he has felt some of that peace, but he explained how he still longed for and prayed for the indescribable peace he briefly felt.

A Morning Conversation

April 26, 1994. Jesus, you woke me up a half hour early. When I tried to go back to sleep I sensed you say, "Sharon, come talk to me. I have something to share with you" (Song 2:13b).

Dear perfect sovereign God, I call you by this name to remind me that you are in total control and perfect in all your ways. But this is a title, not an intimate name. It symbolizes you on a throne, far away, untouched by human anguish. To give me courage to come into your presence this early morning, I will call you loving and merciful sovereign Father. That moves you closer to my heart (Ps. 30:1–2).

And Father, that's the side of you that I need. I need a dad today. One that I trust the way I am accustomed to trusting my own father. He fixed whatever was broken. As a twenty-one-year-old wife, I transferred that father-trust to the man who would become the father of my children. Chuck, my heart, my soulmate. When he enters a room, I feel safe. It seems to me you are asking me to see you as my loving Father in whose lap I am secure and safe.

Lord, I want to be in your lap. I want to rest my head on your chest and feel the peaceful, steady beating of your heart. I long for your strength and to know without a doubt, everything will be OK. How many times did I comfort our own children in this way? How many times was their world safe because their mommy held them on her lap and whispered words of comfort? I rubbed their soft heads, caressed, and kissed their wet tear-stained faces all the while whispering in sing-song rhythm, "I'm here. Your mommy's here. Everything is OK now."

I read the appointed entry in *Streams in the Desert* and in *My Utmost for His Highest*. Chambers's words struck me to the core:

> If we obey what God says according to our sincere belief, God will break us from those traditions that misrepresent Him. There are many such beliefs to be got rid of, e.g., that God removes a child because the mother loves him too much—a devil's lie! and a travesty of the true nature of God. . . .
>
> If you will remain true to God, God will lead you straight through every barrier into the inner chamber of the knowledge of Himself.[1]

O Father, thank you for getting me up early and pulling me into your lap.

I'm Listening, Lord

Several months after Mark's death, a woman from Florida called to invite me to speak at her church women's retreat sched-

uled for the following spring. Tears flowed freely as I told her that
I was not the right person for this task, the grief was too fresh.
The more we talked, the more convinced she was that I should
accept the invitation with the freedom to back out at the last
minute. She encouraged me to see this date as a goal, a test, if
you will, of my progress in this journey through grief.

Chuck agreed that this was a good way to step back into the
speaking ministry. On our ride to the airport we talked about my
theme, Will You Sing at Midnight? and the best way to teach
some of the points. He acknowledged my longing to stay home
and prayed for me to think about the woman in the audience
who was hanging on to life by her fingernails, needing someone
to tell her, "God is faithful, and you can trust him, no matter
how dark your midnight." His parting words at the gate were the
ones he always gave when sending me off to a conference or
retreat, "I love you. Stay on message."

His words rang in my ears every time I stood up to speak. In
my first session I asked the women to turn to Acts 16: the story of
how Paul and Silas responded to severe beatings and unfair
incarceration. Their loud, continuous singing at midnight transformed a dark, dank jail cell into a cathedral where miracles took
place. I told them about the midnight of my life and how I was
struggling to sing praises to God, sometimes out of key, sometimes in a minor key. And then I asked, "Will you sing at midnight?"

On the plane, on my way back home, I sat questioning
whether my proclamation of God's faithful love was even true.
Feeling exhausted, empty, and lonely, I longed for home, and yet
I sadly realized that one child would be missing when I arrived.

*March 3, 1994. Lord, I stepped out by faith, being sure of
what I hope for and certain of what I do not see (Heb. 11:6).
And you empowered me to declare your faithfulness at mid-*

night. But now I'm so weary and empty. I write this and repeat memorized Scriptures and look for hope, but my emotions are screaming at me: cry. Cry out for your son. Lord, how do I walk a steady path in the midst of such conflicting emotions? Sorrow, joy. Laughter, tears. Faith, fear. The war between peace and doubt is fierce. The pathway to peace is not straight but zigzags across the battlefield of life. Only you can give me a steady path. You must give me faith to believe. You must.

Isaiah 26:3: You will keep in perfect peace him whose mind is steadfast, because he trusts in you.

I'm listening, Lord.

"My dear daughter, you will see Mark again. You will see Mark again. I will keep you in perfect peace when your mind is stayed on me. Trust me. Trust me. Trust me. . . . I love you. Let me love you. I love you. Let me love you. Feel my arms around you. Let me love you."

God's tender words invited me to rest from the battle and revel in his love. I picked up the book I had in my carryon, *In My Father's House* by Bodie Thoene, and tried to lose myself in the fictional story. I identified with Birch, a soldier returning from the battlefields of World War I and longing for the security of the past. In a climactic moment, alone in his home church, he pulls out from his pocket an unread letter from his mother. Goosebumps covered my flesh when I read the very words God had given to me just moments before. I recognized other words from my journal that described how I loved Mark. When the author wrote this passage, she did not know that God was writing a love letter to a complete stranger—me:

> [Birch] stood slowly and put his hand on the pocket Bible where Mama's letter waited, still unopened, to speak to his heart in just such a moment of despair. There would be no better time to hear her words. She would have something gentle to say to him. Some word of hope to offer him, an image of heaven beyond the hell of his loneliness! . . .
>
> Closing his eyes he could almost hear her speak. "I told the Lord the day you was born, you're His child, Birch. The Lord is your pa wherever you go. I loved you when you wasn't nothing but a squalling, useless little runt! I loved you and changed your diapers and nursed you when you was hungry. I loved you before you ever plowed a furrow or split one stick of firewood. Hear me now, boy. . . . When you're all alone over there, feeling scared and like your heart's gonna break . . . you remember the Lord loves you even more than I ever could! And He's right there with you. He'll feed your heart when you're hungry, clean you up when you need to be changed! He'll tuck you in when you're cold inside. You just lay yourself in the Lord's arms like a baby, Birch. You don't need to be strong all the time. Let Him love you. He ain't hard on His children."
>
> The voice seemed clear. Had he heard it with his ears or only with his heart? There was no need to open the letter. He could not find the strength to open his eyes, let alone light a candle.
>
> "I'm in need of holdin', Jesus," he whispered. "In need of a Father tonight." And then with a sigh, he fell asleep.[2]

I slowly reread the words, gently closed the book, looked out the window and whispered, "O Jesus, thank you for hearing the cry of my soul. I'm in need of a Father tonight, and I feel you holding me tightly in your grip."

THE TREASURE OF A FATHER'S LOVE

As a father has compassion on his children, so the LORD has compassion on those who fear him; for he knows how we are formed, he remembers that we are dust. (Ps. 103:13–14)

The young woman sat silently in the chair in my sunroom. I recognized the hollow look in her eyes. Her healthy, full-term baby had died the day before her due date. My sweet friend delivered this longed-for daughter knowing she would soon place her little body in a grave. What would help her move beyond bitterness and look forward to experiencing joy once more?

Several years earlier another young woman lay in a hospital bed, waiting for labor to begin so that she could deliver her first-born son, knowing that this loved child had already died in utero. She looked deep into my eyes and asked, "Isn't this mean?" Her question was a cry to reconcile what felt like mean sovereignty with the tender, faithful love of God.

Grief will always shadow these women, but studying the character of God helped them push their sorrow through the grid of his Fatherlove.

Throughout the New Testament God calls those who love Jesus his "sons and daughters": "I will be a Father to you, and you will be my sons and daughters, says the Lord Almighty" (2 Cor. 6:18).

Jesus told Mary Magdalene that his Father is also her Father: "Jesus said, 'Do not hold on to me, for I have not yet returned to the Father. Go instead to my brothers and tell them, "I am returning to my Father and your Father, to my God and your God" ' " (John 20:17).

And Paul exhorts us to remember the sweetness of our Father-child relationship: "For you did not receive a spirit that makes you a slave again to fear, but you received the Spirit of sonship. And by him we cry, 'Abba [daddy], Father' " (Rom. 8:15).

I longed to call God "Daddy" and feel the strength and security such a name represents. I was especially taken by the concept of being "in his grip" versus me holding onto him. In my struggle to reconcile God's Fatherlove with his sovereignty I pictured God's hand wrapped around mine and noted in my journal every Scripture I could find on the hand of God.

After crossing the Red Sea the Israelites sing a song of praise for God's "right hand" raised in majesty, shattering their enemy: "Your right hand, O LORD, was majestic in power. Your right hand, O LORD, shattered the enemy. . . . You stretched out your right hand and the earth swallowed them [gods]. In your unfailing love you will lead the people you have redeemed. In your strength you will guide them to your holy dwelling" (Ex. 15:6, 12–13).

Contrast that description with God's gentle covering of Moses in Exodus 33:22: "When my glory passes by, I will put you in a cleft in the rock and cover you with my hand until I have passed by."

Throughout the Psalms I saw the frequent proclamation of King David's security in knowing God the Father held him by his "right hand," even in the nights of life.

Psalm 16:7–8: "I will praise the LORD, who counsels me; even at night my heart instructs me. I have set the LORD always before me. Because he is at my right hand, I will not be shaken."

Psalm 44:3 reminds me that I won't have victory over the enemies of my soul by pulling myself up by my own bootstraps but through the love of my Father's right hand: "It was not by their sword that they [your children] won the land, nor did their arm bring them victory; it was your right hand, your arm, and the light of your face, for you loved them."

There were times I tried to crawl out of my heavenly Father's lap because I was so disappointed with his actions in my life. But at the same time, I longed for his touch, for the strength of a father's protective hand, and Psalm 63:6–8 became a safe room for me to soak in the Fatherlove of God: "On my bed I remember you; I think of you through the watches of the night. Because you are my help, I sing in the shadow of your wings. My soul clings to you; your right hand upholds me."

When a young bereaved father called our home late one night for comfort, I heard his wife wailing in the background, "I want my baby, please give me my baby." We couldn't give her what she wanted. Instead we agreed that this grief was beyond our ability to carry and that God's actions in their lives appeared to be mean. . . . But as people who had claimed Jesus Christ as Savior, we could come to God as our Father. Without answering our questions, our perfectly wise and good Father asks us to trust his perfect Fatherlove and choose to believe him when he says, "For I am the LORD, your God, who takes hold of your right hand and says to you, Do not fear; I will help you" (Isa. 41:13).

When my circumstances throw into doubt the Fatherlove of God, I picture his strong hand holding mine tightly, his attention never wavering, carefully scoping out the terrain and picking just the right moment to take the next step.

TREASURES OF HOPE

Scriptural Gems

"For you are a people holy to the LORD your God. The LORD your God has chosen you out of all the peoples on the face of the earth to be his people, his treasured possession." (Deut. 7:6)

"But Zion said, 'The LORD has forsaken me, the LORD has forgotten me.' "Can a mother forget the baby at her breast and have no compassion on the child she has borne? Though she may forget, I will not forget you! See, I have engraved you on the palms of my hands; your walls are ever before me.' " (Isa. 49:14–16)

"My sheep listen to my voice; I know them, and they follow me. I give them eternal life, and they shall never perish; no one can snatch them out of my hand. My Father, who has given them to me, is greater than all; no one can snatch them out of my Father's hand." (John 10:27–29)

Songs in the Night: Children of the Heavenly Father
As a young, sickly girl in Sweden, the song's writer, Carolina Sandell Berg, was very close to her pastor father. When she was twenty-six, onboard a ship with him, she watched helplessly as he fell overboard when the vessel suddenly lurched. Rescue efforts failed, and Lina wrote this hymn, which demonstrates the deep eternal love of her heavenly Father.

Children of the heav'nly Father
Safely in his bosom gather;
Nestling bird nor star in heaven
Such a refuge e'er was given.

God his own doth tend and nourish,
In his holy courts they flourish;
From all evil things he spares them,
In his mighty arms he bears them.

Neither life nor death shall ever
From the Lord his children sever;

Unto them his grace he showeth,
And their sorrows all he knoweth.

Praise the Lord in joyful numbers,
Your Protector never slumbers;
At the will of your Defender
Every foeman must surrender.

Though he giveth or he taketh,
God his children ne'er forsaketh;
His the loving purpose solely
To preserve them pure and holy.

More secure is no one ever
Than the loved ones of the Savior;
Not yon star on high abiding
Nor the bird in home-nest hiding.

Other Hopeful Ideas

In your journal describe ways that you can see God fathering you.

Hosea 11:3 gives a fascinating image of God, as Father: "It was I who taught Ephraim to walk, taking them by the arms." Imagine yourself in this parental role. Then imagine yourself as a child, allowing God to help you learn to walk. Journal any new insights about this aspect of God's parental love—and the role of his hands.

Review the Scriptures in this chapter and list how each one reveals his Fatherlove. God my Father is my Protector . . . Helper . . . and so forth. Your emotions may scream against what you see. Remember that it takes time for the medication of God's Word to reduce the inflammation of a broken heart. Choose by faith to believe what God says about his Fatherlove even though you can't fit all the puzzle pieces together.

Prayer: Your Invitation

O God, we are so frail without hope unless you father us through the blood of your Son, Jesus. Father, open our ears to your invitation to crawl up into your lap and let you love us. Amen.

12

$\mathscr{I}$T'S $\mathscr{N}$OT ABOUT $\mathscr{M}$E

THE TREASURE OF PURPOSE

 MIDNIGHT PRINCIPLE: My circumstances are my platform for glorifying God.

JOURNAL INSIGHT

October 3, 1994, Sandy Cove Writer's Conference.
Lord, the only reason I'm here is because friends gave
me this gift. People are friendly, but I am so lonely,
trapped in a private club no one else wants to join. I have
heard dramatic stories today of children saved from torna-
does and deadly diseases. And I'm thrilled for their par-

ents, but you did not save my son from death. I long for
Mark.

O God, I know you have an eternal purpose, but I live
in a finite world. I feel you drawing me to Jeremiah 29:11. Is
this Scripture really for me? "For I know the plans I have
for you. Plans to prosper you and not to harm you. Plans to
give you a hope and a future. Then you will call upon me and
come and pray to me and I will listen to you. You will seek
me and find me when you seek me with all your heart. I will
be found by you. I will bring you back from captivity."

And Psalm 81, especially verse 10: "I am the LORD your
God, who brought you up out of Egypt. Open wide your mouth and
I will fill it." And verse 11. "But my people would not listen to me;
Israel would not submit to me." Am I refusing your treasures?
Your healing? Or am I right where I should be in this journey?

And verses 13–14: "If my people would but listen to me,
If Israel would follow my ways, how quickly would I subdue
their enemies and turn my hand against their foes."

Lord, what are you saying to me? Am I resisting your
voice? I'm listening, Lord.

YOU HAVE WORK TO DO

An Intimate Response

Someone told us that the second year of grief after the sudden loss of a child is often worse than the first. After the first-year

anniversary of Mark's death, changing seasons marked off the ever-widening realization of unending losses. School buses, back-to-school sales, high school athletic teams practicing for fall sports—everywhere I looked were reminders that we had been raped by death. Mark should have been enjoying his senior year of high school. Instead, I was trying to find that "new level of normal." Life often felt obscene.

A friend told me that my skin was gray. Chuck told me he hated the pain in my eyes even when I was laughing. I think that circles of pain radiated from me, and it was difficult for people to be around me.

Concerned friends encouraged me to deepen my writing skills and sent me to a writer's conference. The investment of these precious friends took on great value as God intimately responded to the cries of my soul. My first night, alone in my room I wrote in my journal the entry at the beginning of the chapter. . . . "I'm listening, Lord."

I continued to write, what I sensed to be God's response.

Sharon, I have a plan, a purpose (Jer. 29:11). Mark's death is not an accident. Mark is alive. Do you hear me? Will you listen to me? Will you believe me? Will you trust me with your child? Mark is fine. Can you let him go? Can you imagine my joy when I welcomed him home? Can you accept my call to you? My purpose for you? Can you step back and rest in me? Trust that I do have a plan that was not to harm you but to prosper you? Remember my idea of prosperity is different from yours and the world's. My idea of prosperity is to bring you into intimacy with me. Keep seeking me and you will find me (1 Chron. 28:9). Isn't that what you want? Don't you want your children close to me? I know you miss him, Sharon. I created you to miss him. But one day when you're with me, you'll look back and say, "Now I understand and God does all things well."

Don't waste your time. Use it. Use it to build my kingdom and to equip the Body of Christ that I have called you to. You have work to do. It is my work. You will one day look back at your life and you will exclaim, "Only God could have done this."

Watch me. Look for me everywhere (see Ps. 139; Job). I'm working in ways you don't know. Watch me. You will see the puzzle parts come together. Watch me work. Look for me in everything you do. Trust me to write through you. There is a person who needs to hear my words through you as my vessel.

Obey me. Trust me.

Listen to me.

I am holding on to you.

Mark is safely in my grip.

I love him.

I love you.

Let me love you.

Trust me.

You have work to do.

Open wide your mouth.
Watch me fill it.
It breaks my heart when you refuse my blessings.
Watch me bring healing.
Watch me.

After writing this wonderful message from God, I turned out the lights and sobbed. I knew God was calling me to surrender to his love, yet I could feel the ghost of grief prowling, stalking, preparing to move in for the kill. In the darkness, I whispered Mark's name and then Jesus'. "Oh, Mark, I miss you. How I love you. Jesus, you are my Deliverer. You are my Hope. You are my Helper. Help me, help me."

On the Home Front

Chuck knew that my attendance at the conference was a walk of faith and that I was limping badly. He urged me to sleep at home the second night and return for the meetings the next morning.

After we turned out the lights at bedtime, Chuck held me and told me he asked me to come home because he couldn't stand to be alone. *He's going down, and he can't stop. Lord, how he is struggling and wants to quit.* He said he would quit the ministry if we weren't depending on him.

October 4, morning. How can I help him? I'm so broken myself. He is so much stronger than he knows, because you are filling his emptiness. Lord, I see your strength glowing in the cracks of this clay pot. He says every step is a step in the darkness, taken by faith. I told him that you must be very pleased with him because without faith it is impossible to please you.

Watch Me Work

October 4, evening. You told me yesterday to watch you work. And I am. At every meal, in every seminar, I am meeting women who have lost children through horrific circumstances. Each meeting introduces me to your daughters who are choosing to walk by faith in darkness. Their eyes are filled with pain, but laughter lines frame their faces.

Tonight, Chuck joined me for dinner at the conference and we chose to go hear Don Wyrtzen, one of the seminar speakers who is also a writer and musician. We thought we were going to a concert. Instead he preached. And, O Lord, how we watched you work.

Don talked about the power of music when it is wedded to God's Word. He had us turn to Colossians 3 and Ephesians 5 to show how music counsels us. But when he turned to Acts 16:16–40 my heart beat faster; I sensed God was about to do something just for us. I whispered to Chuck, "This is my passage, the one I based my seminar on—you know, Will You Sing at Midnight?"

Don described Paul and Silas with the same words I use in my seminars.

He asked, "Why didn't they rage against God? How could they sing?" He described the horror of their beatings. Yet they sang. How could they sing? Because they were filled with the Spirit, as described in Ephesians 5, they could sing at midnight.

Don's next story demonstrated the power of music in a contemporary setting. A woman told him that his song "And the Father Said Goodbye" had saved her marriage. Her only child, six years old, had been hit by a car in front of their home. His dad had come home from work early and turned the corner just in time to witness the death of his son. They froze in their grief and withdrew from life. Where was God?

Their choir director came to them and said, "We don't know how you feel, but we are your family. We are your brothers and sisters. We want you to come and sit in the choir while we practice. You don't have to sing. Just sit in the middle of us and just let us be with you." To get the choir director off their backs, they eventually went to the rehearsals. The choir was preparing Christmas music, including Wyrtzen's song, which is a description of God saying farewell to his only Son on the threshold of heaven, coming to earth. These grieving parents changed the words to reflect them saying farewell to their son as he entered heaven. That moment was the beginning of their healing.

Don mentioned his feeling of helplessness when talking to people carrying overwhelming grief—such as a mother whose eight-year-old daughter had died of leukemia; this mother had not cried in nine years. He encouraged her to be Jewish in her sorrow and, like David, wail in the presence of God. He said that Psalm 23 indicates that God walks with us in the dark night of the soul.

October 4. O Father, Don Wrytzen did not know our journey, he did not know about Mark, but you designed his message with us in mind. As we walked back to my hotel room after the service, I told Chuck, "If he had said, 'God's grace is not an anesthetic, it doesn't remove the pain' then I would know this is a supernatural moment and I'd wait for the lightning from God's hand."

Later that evening we introduced ourselves to Don during a refreshment break. We told him about Mark and Kelly and how much his message meant to us. Without any prompting from us, he attempted to soothe our obvious heartbreak with the words "God's grace is not an anesthetic. It doesn't remove the pain."

Lord, it's as if you said, "What else can I do for you? OK, want more? Here. Now do you believe I'm here?"

Don kept saying, "I don't know why this has happened to you but when you wake up in the middle of the night and it's dark and you're scared and Mark is gone, remember: Jesus is with you. Hold on. Give yourself time. God has something special. You are very special. He has a special purpose for you even though you may not want it."

Chuck was very moved. He said it was like God had lit a fire. He told me to write it all down before I forgot one detail.

O Lord, we are on holy ground. We have to step back and catch our breath. What are you doing?

October 5, morning. I spent the night here by myself because I didn't want to miss any morning session. As I sat at breakfast I realized that the conference is over. But you have been orchestrating such dramatic treasures in the darkness that I *concluded I am still here for one more gift. So I prayed, "Lord, if there is one more person you want me to talk to and that's why I'm here, I'm listening."*

A few minutes later, Christine Tangveld, a children's author and conference speaker, approached me and said, "I haven't had a chance to talk to you, but please don't leave this place without seeing me."

After breakfast, in the lounge, she explained that Don had told the staff our story. She felt she had a message for me that could be life-changing. Her son had died nine years earlier. Seeing my eyes fill with tears, she exclaimed, "See, I can say that and still smile!"

Then she dramatically portrayed God's message for me.

She stood up in front of me and started walking in place. "We're all in a lifeline," she said. "It begins at birth. We're walking along and life is great. Then something terrible happens. My son died. So I turned my back on my future and I faced that horrible event. 'I can't turn my back on my son,' I said. 'I can't let go of my son.'"

Tears streamed down my cheeks as her words wrapped around my wounded heart. She continued, " 'If I let go, who will remember him? Will I remember how he looks? His voice? If I let go, I'm saying it's OK that he's gone. And it's not OK. I'm angry. I hate life. My job is to make people remember him.' So for a long time, I refused to face today or tomorrow. I planted my feet in yesterday. But then a friend said, 'Christine, your son is not back here.' She pointed toward the floor. 'Your son is up there, waiting for you.' She pointed toward the sky. 'He's cheering you on, saying, "Come on, Mom. You have work to do. Come on, you can do it." '

"I hated what she was saying, but I knew she was right. It took me three days to physically turn from this horrible event and face the future. But picturing my son at the end of this physical lifeline, in heaven, part of the great cloud of witnesses, cheering me on, reminding me that God can be trusted, that it's all true, that gives me freedom to live life as God has purposed for me."

O God, she used the exact words you spoke to me in my journal. "You have work to do."

"Watch me," you say.

Lord, I'm watching.

The Treasure of Purpose

"As long as it is day, we must do the work of him who sent me." (John 9:4)

About two years after Mark's death, I prayed that God would reveal his heart to me, admitting that I still didn't know him as I longed to. I heard him respond, "If you want to know me, get to know my Son. Walk with him on the dusty roads of Galilee. Watch the way he interacts with people. Learn what drives him. Then you will get a glimpse into my heart, because my Son and I are One."

For the next year, I lived in the book of John. And I fell more in love with Jesus. I learned that every act of God is intentional and that his purposes will stand. No matter how quickly Jesus could have relieved pain for others, he did so only when it would further the purposes of his Father in heaven. He often reminded people that he had come to do the will of his Father and nothing would deter him from accomplishing his life purpose.

Walking with Jesus through the words of John helped me better understand the mind of God and his plans for my life. Jesus' response to his disciples when they asked why a certain man had been born blind gave deeper meaning to Mark's death and an eternal purpose for my life: "Neither this man nor his parents sinned," said Jesus, "but this happened so that the work of God might be displayed in his life" (John 9:3). I'd previously noted this verse, but now I saw that it was followed by a challenge. "As long as it is day, we must do the work of him who sent me. Night is coming, when no one can work" (John 9:4).

I began to see this message again and again through the Scriptures. Yes, my dreams were gone. My plans shattered. But God's were still intact. Like Jesus, as long as it was day, I had work to do. But I still did not understand what work I could do in my broken state.

One day in the winter of 1996 I was home alone and longing for a friend. I didn't have anything new to say to any of my trusted confidantes, so this seemed to be a moment when God wanted me to reach out to a long-distance mentor. I built a fire, curled up under an afghan, and picked up a book by Susan Hunt, a personal friend and the head of our denomination's women's ministries. I pleaded with God to speak specifically to me. I don't remember which book it was, but as I finished the last page, I took away this message: *Your circumstances are your platform for glorifying God.*

I had never heard it put quite that way before. What was my platform? Daily life in the context of the death of my child. My task was to determine the best way to honor God in these circumstances. I did have specific work to do. The promise of Ephesians 2:10 gave me confidence that before time began God had planned out this pathway for me and that he had good works to be completed by me: "For we are God's workmanship, created in Christ Jesus to do good works, which God prepared in advance for us to do."

The riches of Scripture reminded me that my life was not over because of Mark's death. And your life is not over because of your loss. Just as Mark's days were ordained by God before one of them came to be (Ps. 139:16b), so were mine and so are yours. He promised to direct my steps as I called on him. My responsibility continues to be to open wide my mouth. His responsibility is to fill it. ("I am the LORD your God, who brought you up out of Egypt. Open wide your mouth and I will fill it" [Ps. 81:10].) Seeing my circumstances as my platform for glorifying God gave me a place to start with everyday life. I became more intentional in the way I responded to the tasks before me. They had meaning.

Can you accept your circumstances as a platform for glorifying God? Do you resist such a plan, because to do so seems to let God off the hook for your anguish? If so, ask God to help you pray with the psalmist: "Not to us, O LORD, not to us, but to your name be the glory, because of your love and faithfulness" (Ps. 115:1).

TREASURES OF HOPE

Scriptural Gems

Soaking in the truth of God's character will energize you for the tasks ahead. Tell God how you are feeling and ask him to confront your feelings with his truth. Spend some time soaking in the following Scriptures and ask God to open your heart and mind to his deep love and presence. To give you strength, own the character of God described in these passages. For example, Psalm 68:19 promises that God daily bears our burdens. When the task of glorifying God in your circumstances threatens to undo you, cry out to him, "You are *my* Burden Bearer in this moment, Lord." Notice that I didn't say, "Be my Burden Bearer." I acknowledge with my words that he *is* my Burden Bearer. Write each one of these phrases on a 3 x 5 card and place them in strategic spots around your home or workplace. When you are ready to fall apart, choose to pray one of these phrases:

You are *my* God. (Ps. 81:10)

You are *my* Helper. You are *my* Consolation. (Ps. 94:14, 17–19)

You are *my* Burden Bearer. (Ps. 68:19–20)

You are *my* Rest, *my* Rock, *my* Rescue, *my* Refuge. (Ps. 62:1–2)

"And God is able to make all grace abound to you, so that in all things at all times, having all that you need, you will abound in every good work." (2 Cor. 9:8)

Note also the Scriptures mentioned earlier in the chapter, particularly Jeremiah 29:11 and John 9:3–4.

Songs in the Night: Day by Day

Carolina Sandell Berg, the Swedish hymn writer who wrote "Children of the Heavenly Father" after seeing her father drown, later penned this favorite hymn, reminding her, and us, that our heavenly Father sustains us moment by moment, day by day. I especially love the second verse, which reminds me of God's sweet enabling presence in the darkness. He never expects me to accomplish his work without equipping me to do so.

Day by day and with each passing moment,
Strength I find to meet my trials here;
Trusting in my Father's wise bestowment,
I've no cause for worry or for fear.
He whose heart is kind beyond all measure
Gives unto each day what he deems best—
Lovingly, its part of pain and pleasure,
Mingling toil with peace and rest.

Every day the Lord himself is near me
With a special mercy for each hour;
All my cares he fain would bear, and cheer me,
He whose name is Counselor and Pow'r.
The protection of his child and treasure
Is a charge that on himself he laid;
"As your days, your strength shall be in measure,"
This the pledge to me he made.

Help me then in every tribulation
So to trust thy promises, O Lord,
That I lose not faith's sweet consolation
Offered me within your holy Word.
Help me, Lord, when toil and trouble meeting,
E'er to take, as from a father's hand,
One by one, the days, the moments fleeting,
Till I reach the promised land.[1]

Other Hopeful Ideas

Continue to journal what you hear God saying to you in your quiet times. Note how in this chapter I sometimes journaled what I thought God was saying in response to my pleas for help. Then I noted the Scriptures from which the message came. This way I knew that his Word was guiding me—not my imagination.

Try to articulate one or two ways in which your circumstances are your platform for glorifying God. Put another way, how has your grief changed your life work or even become your life work, changing the way you relate to and minister to other people facing pain?

For one week, at the end of each day try to write down some effort you've taken to turn your grief—even if it's in some very small way—into a work that God can use.

Prayer: Grief Work as Labor

O Father, this is a difficult place to be, seeing our grief work as labor that can glorify you. You are our Burden Bearer, our Helper, our Deliverer just for this moment. Give us eyes and a heart that accept our circumstances as our platforms to glorify you, and show us the eternal work that waits for us today.

13

$\mathscr{P}$ERMISSION
TO $\mathscr{E}$NJOY

THE TREASURE OF APPRECIATING BEAUTY

MIDNIGHT PRINCIPLE: I can give myself permission to find comfort in—even enjoy—God's creation, which provides glimpses of God's heavenly kingdom.

JOURNAL INSIGHT

March 7, 1995. I watched the sun rise in Kauai and read Job 38–42.

Lord, piece by piece you are dismantling my demand for control, for understanding. I long to respond to your creation confrontation with the words of Job, "My ears had heard of you, but now my eyes have seen you" (42:5).

Perhaps pain is becoming my friend. It opens my eyes to the reality of your character. But such revelation requires a choice. Your creation demands a heart response. It begs the question: Who did this? . . . My surroundings force me to look into your eyes and listen carefully. "Look at me! See the boundaries of the mighty ocean. The order of creation. The boundless brilliant stars scattered over a black, velvet carpet. Can you bind Pleiades or loose the cords of Orion? Can you stop spring from following winter?" (see Job 38–41).

I felt you call me to your heart while it was still dark so I tiptoed out onto the lanai, Bible and journal in hand. Early morning darkness slowly gave way to a crown of sunlight that framed the clouds. Strong breezes swept away the clouds for the glorious entrance of the sun, so brilliant I couldn't look at it (see Job 37:21).

A few years ago a hurricane swept over this island and destroyed everything man had erected. What man makes can be demolished in less than a second. It's only because of your control that the world has boundaries. You stand astride the earth, power and strength sheathed in a sword by your side. That is majesty.

Your fingerprints are everywhere. Chuck pointed out the sliver of moon rising above the just setting sun. "That's majesty," he said.

How can anyone believe this just happened?

By change and only by chance, as one tourist sign proclaimed?

Roots suck up the tropical rains. Brilliant colors push their way into multi-shaded foliage. Deep reds, purples, blues, yellows, orange. The bird-of-paradise flower perches among dark green leaves. This is all by chance? Please! Red-capped birds, plumed, colorful parrots, even the funny roosters running wild. By chance? Never. God, you describe your power, your might, your majesty, your balance, your order. The protections built into your creation. Your sovereignty. And then you demand a response from my platform of ultimate, deep, excruciating, blinding, gripping, helpless, hopeless grief and pain and anguish and suffering. You demand an answer.

You even address the issues of death: "Have the gates of death been shown to you? Have you seen the gates of the shadow of death?" (Job 38:17).

And again, Lord, you shout, "Look at me. Look into my eyes. Will you trust me? I have walked the valley of the shadow of death. And I proclaim victory and restoration. I proclaim new life! Life is impossible without death. Life is impossible without darkness, dampness. Sharon, there is a hard shell restraining you from experiencing all I have planned for you. While you are on this earth, you will struggle to break out of that shell. Only when that shell is broken through death will you be free, free, free. But your time is not yet. For now, you have work to do. Work that will bring hope and freedom to others. Work that will prepare them to face the shadow of death here on this fallen earth. As you work, give yourself permission to enjoy the beauty of fallen earth. Soak it in. Use every sense. Breathe deeply the exquisite aroma dripping from exotic, tropical flowers. Let the scent of the gardenias turn your heart toward me. Listen closely for the cacophony of song. The lone chirping of a single bird. See the brilliant colors that man did not create: fuschia, magenta, brilliant reds, golds, varied blues of the sky. Soak up the tufts of clouds, some like white cotton candy or others like mounds of whipped cream, waiting for a child's finger! Experience the changing colors of the sea, the heat of the bubbling hot white, glowing lava, the warmth of the early morning sun, the cool of the ocean. Enjoy my world.

"Sharon, my daughter, I did this. Can I not sustain and care for you, my child?"

GIVE YOURSELF PERMISSION

A Cross in the Night

With that special, intimate time fresh in my heart, every sense was on full alert as we navigated the winding mountainous roads of Hawaii. I didn't want to miss one treasure, one moment that God had prepared to draw me more tightly into his heart. As we meandered along the road, making frequent stops to take in the sights, I told Chuck about a treasure God had revealed to me the night before.

Several hours into the night, I suddenly woke up. I thanked God for our congregation that had given us this twenty-fifth anniversary gift, a trip to Hawaii. We had thought that by waiting a year to take the trip, we would be more ready to enjoy it. But sorrow was our constant companion, and we had to choose to enjoy our surroundings. That night we had opened wide the ceiling-to-floor windows so that the soft sounds of the pounding surf would rock us to sleep. I felt drawn to stare at the black, velvet sky and the stunning, brilliant, glittering stars, each one named by God. Slowly, they took on shape. I squinted to be sure of what I saw. Yes, on the canvas of the massive sky that reached from the farthest brink of the universe to the tip of the ocean, was a constellation of stars that formed an enormous cross. I held my breath and didn't move. In that moment, I felt the Creator God condescend to my level and sit on the edge of my bed. The cross reminded me of the ultimate act of his love. He gave me the song of the empty cross that night (Ps. 42:8). Peace covered me like a warm afghan, and the next thing I remember, the sun invited me to enjoy another glorious day.

Akaka Falls

The signs in the parking lot at Akaka Falls cautioned us to lock our car and to view the sights at our own risk. Such a warning didn't make us feel welcome, but one of the tourist books had recommended this site so we were determined to see it. We took our time walking up the mountain pathway. Scents of moist, tropical earth and exotic flowers blanketed us. We were emotionally and physically overcome with a sense of anticipation. Everywhere we looked we saw another wonder of God's creation. Chuck picked a pink orchid and tucked it behind my ear. Only one other couple stood on the platform, high in the mountain, facing Akaka Falls.

The beauty found its way into every pore. I was light-headed with the enormity of God's presence. This was a treasure in the darkness. God was there in a way that I had never before experienced. We talked quietly about the gardens we had visited right before this stop. Signs had proudly exclaimed that they were nature tamed and controlled by man. Cascading water falls spilled into well-kept ponds. We had seen the gardeners pick every dead leaf, maintain the crystal clear pools, and care for the fish in the ponds. We couldn't find any weeds on the manicured grounds. We agreed that this was a taste of the Garden of Eden and a foretaste of heaven.

We leaned quietly against the railings and watched the tons of foaming, splashing water crash down from hundreds of feet. The rushing water, singing birds, rustling leaves created an intimate, private sanctuary.

In my heart I whispered, *Mark, is this what you are experiencing? Is your lean, muscular, manly body diving fearlessly from the edge of a cliff into cool, clear, clean waters? Do you have a supernatural appreciation for the eternal, ethereal beauty surrounding you? Is God giving me a foretaste of heaven? I can't imagine your joy at this very moment. For the first time since you left us, I am not sad but I am crying. Can you see my tears as I imagine you experiencing all of Jesus? Complete, content, satisfied in him. What does that mean? Mark, I feel you right here next to me. Are you here? God is. And you are with him, so. . . .*"

My journal record of this moment ended with this comment to God:

O God, you know I'm not trying to talk to Mark, not really. That's impossible and wrong. I am just trying to express my heart. And today, Lord, you gave me a treasure in the darkness that I will cherish forever. You gave me a sense of heaven, of what it means to be forever in your presence. I will never forget this moment.

THE TREASURE OF APPRECIATING BEAUTY

I lift up my eyes to the hills—where does my help come from? My help comes from the LORD, the Maker of heaven and earth. (Ps. 121:1–2)

Before this trip to Hawaii, the year after Mark's death, Chuck and I sat on the deck of my sister's home in Idaho, surrounded by the Grand Tetons. We read to each other chapters in Job, in which God challenges Job to look at creation and see his God. As we read, we saw how every aspect of nature revealed to us a character quality of God and reminded us of his omnipotence and presence.

Even so, Chuck and I waited a year before we took the trip to Hawaii because we were too weary to travel, let alone enjoy such breathtaking surroundings. From experience I know how grief work saps one's energy. Choosing to appreciate any beauty may be more than you can handle right now, but keep reading.

The beauty of nature is a treasure crafted by God. Ever since the day sin slammed shut the door to the Garden of Eden, weeds, disease, bugs, drought, too much rain—all work against the beauty of creation. And yet his creation speaks: "Since the creation of the world God's invisible qualities—his eternal power and divine nature—have been clearly seen, being understood from what has been made, so that men are without excuse" (Rom. 1:20). Unfortunately many people abuse the treasure of creation. Instead of allowing it to draw them into the heart of God, they make idols of the gifts of God (Rom. 1:25). But grace shines through for the child of God, and he continues to uncover "riches stored in secret places" through the beauty of his earth.

He can use beauty to soothe our inflamed souls. The inflammation of grief opens up senses that might not normally fully notice such a treasure. Try sitting by a river on a warm fall day and listen to the softly lapping waves, the chattering of birds. Watch a fuzzy spider skitter across a tiny stick, observe the soaring seagulls, breathe in the scent of a sweet flower, or touch the prickly thorns of a rose. And let each sensation lead you into the heart of your creator God. Appreciate such exquisite beauty and realize these gifts are only a shadow of the eternal beauty that God is preparing for each of his children in heaven.

The writers of Scripture often exclaimed that they saw God's fingerprints throughout creation. Some of David's most beautiful psalms reflect the hours of solitude he spent as a shepherd, meditating on his surroundings, appreciating God's handiwork and allowing God to speak to him through it (note Ps. 121:1–2; Ps. 8; Ps. 19; Ps. 98).

About a year into our grief journey I decided that I would intentionally laugh out loud at anything fun or joyful. I would choose to enjoy the tiniest glimpse of beauty. My goal was to one day use as much energy to laugh as to wail. It seemed important to give myself permission to enjoy the beauty of life and to force my atrophied laugh and joy muscles to work once more.

John Keats said, "A thing of beauty is a joy forever." In time you'll know that he's right. Give yourself permission to enjoy a bit of beauty today.

TREASURES OF HOPE

Scriptural Gems

As I said, choosing to appreciate any beauty may be more than you can handle right now. Tuck away the promises of these

Scriptures and trust that at some point, you will give yourself permission to enjoy and rest in the signs of hope and glimpses of heaven through God's creation.

"See! The winter is past; the rains are over and gone. Flowers appear on the earth; the season of singing has come, the cooing of doves is heard in our land. The fig tree forms its early fruit; the blossoming vines spread their fragrance. Arise, come, my darling; my beautiful one, come with me." (Song 2:11–13)

"He will yet fill your mouth with laughter and your lips with shouts of joy." (Job 8:21)

We think of "Joy to the World" as a Christmas song. But it really is a loose paraphrase of Psalm 98. "Let heaven and nature sing." Think of Psalm 98:8: "Let the rivers clap their hands, let the mountains sing together for joy; let them sing before the LORD."

Joseph chose to see his son Ephraim as a symbol of God's beauty and named him accordingly: "The second son he named Ephraim and said, 'It is because God has made me fruitful in the land of my suffering.' " (Gen. 41:52)

"I waited patiently for the LORD. He turned to me and heard my cry. He lifted me out of the slimy pit, out of the mud and mire; he set my feet on a rock and gave me a firm place to stand. He put a new song in my mouth, a hymn of praise to our God. Many will see and fear and put their trust in the LORD." (Ps. 40:1–3)

Songs in the Night: This Is My Father's World
This song was written in the late nineteenth century by Malthie Babcock, a Presbyterian pastor in Baltimore and then New York City. I especially like the third verse, which acknowl-

edges the imperfection of this life and looks forward to the future redemption of heaven and earth.

> This is my Father's world, and to my list'ning ears,
> All nature sings, and round me rings the music of the
>> spheres.
> This is my Father's world: I rest me in the thought
> Of rocks and trees, of skies and seas; his hand the won-
>> ders wrought.
>
> This is my Father's world, the birds their carols raise,
> The morning light, the lily white, declare their Maker's
>> praise.
> This is my Father's world: he shines in all that's fair;
> In the rustling grass I hear him pass, he speaks to me
>> everywhere.
>
> This is my Father's world, O let me ne'er forget
> That though the wrong seems oft so strong, God is the
>> ruler yet.
> This is my Father's world: The battle is not done;
> Jesus who died shall be satisfied, and earth and heav'n
>> be one.

Other Hopeful Ideas

Review the Scriptures above and note in your journal how nature (flowers blooming, doves singing) symbolizes healing, joy, a new day.

In the morning, write out in your journal this sentence: "Lord, open my eyes to one glimpse of your creation that will soothe the inflammation of my heart or make me laugh out loud."

Look for his response not only in the creation of the earth and its contents but also in the creative arts of people. Take note of photographs, paintings, the engineering or architectural genius evident in a bridge or skyscraper. Go for a walk and breathe in the air, notice the cloud formations. All of this may sound a little silly if you are fresh in your grief. But at some point, you will grow tired of your pain and long for a way to climb out of the abyss. These are small steps that will help turn your heart toward the God of all comfort.

Outside my office window on this bitterly cold day, I see an empty bird's nest high in the branches of the leafless maple tree. And I thank God that spring is coming; birds will fly out of that tree and visit the feeder situated outside our kitchen window. Even the day's snow-threatening clouds turn my heart toward the promise of springtime when goldfinches will make our back yard their home. I look forward to considering the magnificence of the tiny hummingbirds—all created by our perfect, loving, always present God.

Why do such musings and meditations turn our hearts toward the love of God? Evelyn Bence puts it well in this reflective prayer:

> I'm not sure I understand how two hours in an art museum with a friend—pushing a stroller, even—can open up one's closed-in world. We rehash our old themes—loves, labors, losses—and the art puts them in perspective. Our here-and-now is connected to the there-and-then. Light breaking in. Water breaking over. Sweat breaking out.
>
> God, Scripture says you have put eternity in our hearts. Help us enlarge the frame in which we see our lives.[1]

Write a prayer of your own, asking God to enlarge your view of his world.

Prayer: The Gifts of Beauty

Father of creation, give us strength to intentionally open our hands to receive the gifts of beauty surrounding us. Teach us how to laugh again and experience deep joy when we reflect on these symbols of your love.

14

CALL BACK

THE TREASURE OF THINKING
AND ACTING BIBLICALLY

MIDNIGHT PRINCIPLE: Thinking biblically encourages me to live biblically, ultimately leading me to reach out to others.

JOURNAL INSIGHT

November 18, 1994. I want to give up. Please let me give up. I'm tired of trying to be good, of trying to honor you. I'm sick of trying to live in a world full of shattered lives.

I seek help from the story of Elijah. He asked you hard questions. You answered him. Why won't you answer us? Scripture declares that the battle belongs to the Lord. I don't know what that means! I don't know how to let you fight my battles. . . .

I see the relentless power you display and cry out, "When will you display your power with lightning and fire in our lives?"

The strong man Elijah's weakness in the face of such power terrifies me. How I can expect to be strong when such a man faltered? Elijah witnessed fire from heaven, licking up the water and burning the soaked sacrifices, and he still suffered from depression, despair, and loneliness. How can this be? What does it take to be healed?

We are well into the second year and I still wail. I have no hope of ever being healed. A new level of normal—adjust to life without Mark. Unbelievable. Crazy. Stupid. Idiotic. Insane. Unfair. Excruciating. Torture. Loneliness. Betrayal.

The clock just keeps ticking. The pendulum swings, swings, swings, swings. Tick, tick, tick, tick. I miss Mark.

You spoke to Elijah in a gentle whisper. You reminded him of his responsibility to your church. You told him to go back the way he came, to your people and to fulfill his responsibilities as your prophet. He was to pass on the legacy of leadership to the next generation. O God, what is my responsibility to the next generation? What should I do to fill my days? Whisper to me.

November 21, 1994. Dear Lord, Chuck woke up early Sunday morning and started walking the neighborhood, telling you that he did not intend to show up at church. Then a still, gentle voice. "Chuck, pray, pray for your neighbors. You must keep stepping outside of yourself to find me. Do as Job did. Pray for your neighbors." And as he walked, he prayed for each family.

In his sermon Chuck admitted this to the congregation. Hearing Chuck's story, I heard your voice reminding me of who I am in you, of the privilege of serving you, challenging me, "Hold on. Hold on. Hold on. Commit your heart to me." Hold on based on what the Scriptures teach about you, not what my heart is screaming. Not what my circumstances are wailing. Hold on.

O Father, I don't understand, but I know you are not asking me to understand. You are asking, demanding, that I trust and obey. Perhaps it's in the obedience that I will understand more of you. You created me. You know how weak I am. You know how hard this is. How impossible. How painful. You must give me the power to choose.

Daniel's friend sent him a note, and I clutch it as your response to me: "Humble yourselves, therefore, under God's mighty hand, that he may lift you up in due time. Cast all your anxiety on him because he cares for you" (1 Peter 5:6–7).

With my will, I choose to believe that you care for me. I will trust and obey.

CALLING BACK

It was 1996, the week before our fourth Thanksgiving without Mark. For the first time since losing our son I thought I had prepared myself for the holiday season. I was actually looking forward to going to the mall to hear our choir sing. Then I got a phone call.

"Sharon, I'm so sorry to call you with this news, but there is another pastor's family that has just lost their son in a terrible accident." It was my friend Susan. I knew what she would want me to do. I didn't think I could. Suddenly darkness shattered the little bit of light that was carrying me through the holiday season.

Susan continued. "Mike and Leslie Singenstreu serve a church in Illinois. They have four children and were waiting for their oldest child, fifteen-year-old Zach, to come home from work. The table was set for dinner. Zach was late. Mike got worried so he went to look for him." Susan's voice broke when she concluded, "Mike found Zach at the accident scene. Zach was hit by a truck as he was riding his bike home from his job."

Although I had never met Zach's parents, I knew them better at this moment than they knew themselves. In a split second, without warning, death shattered this family that faithfully served our God and his people. Their lives would never be the same. Never.

"Sharon, Leslie sounds just like you did. Mike is a faithful pastor, and he needs Chuck."

I didn't want to talk to Leslie. I didn't want her fresh grief to blow down my carefully constructed house of holiday cards. I had intentionally chosen to enjoy the holidays, just this little bit.

"Susan, some people don't want to speak to other bereaved parents. We're strangers. Why don't you just give them our phone number and tell them to call us when they are ready?"

Susan didn't seem to hear my words. "They need to talk to you now. How about if I call Leslie and ask her the best time for you to call her?"

Reluctantly, I told Susan all right.

I hung up the phone and walked outside, crying. "Lord, you know how hard I've planned and prepared for this season. You know I want to honor you and the birth of your Son. Why must I go back into the midnight darkness right now? I don't think I can do this. I can't do this."

Then God reminded me of those who had willingly gone back into their own sorrow in order to help us. He played back the words I had written in my journal where I had prayed that some day I would hold a brokenhearted mother in my arms and tell her that God is faithful and that she could trust him, even in her grief. I concluded that if God was calling me to this friendship of encouragement, he would enable me to give Leslie whatever she needed.

I heard the phone ring, took a deep breath, and went back inside. It was Susan again. She could barely speak through her sobs. "Oh, Sharon, Leslie sounds just like you did in the first days after you lost Mark. She wants you to call her. Sharon, I know that what I am asking you to do is incredibly sacrificial. I'm going to pray more for you as you reach out to Leslie than I am even for Leslie over the next few hours." Susan sobbed uncontrollably as we hung up the phones. My eyes were dry.

OK, Lord. I'll try. At the appointed hour, I dialed the number Susan had given me. I expected to fall apart the minute Leslie answered the phone, but I did not shed a tear during our conversation. I recognized Leslie's weak and lifeless voice. Yes, she sounded like me. Leslie told me that she had heard me speak about my journey in grief at a women's conference. When her friends had wanted to speak to me afterwards, Leslie had told them that she didn't want to meet me or know me. She was afraid that she would lose her own son; getting close to me would make that fear more real. As we closed our phone conversation, I started to say, "Leslie, I know that nothing I have said to you has made you feel better but . . ."

Leslie stopped me. "Wait. Your voice is strong. That gives me hope that one day my voice will be strong again."

A *Supernatural Exchange*

I thought later about this strange comment and realized that God had performed a supernatural exchange. As she had promised, Susan had gathered several friends together to pray during my conversation with Leslie. I believe God gave Susan my tears so that I could be for Leslie what she needed for that moment. I could not fix Leslie; only God could do that. But Leslie needed hope, and hearing another bereaved mother speak with a strong voice gave her hope that one day she, too, would be strong again. When I later reminded Leslie of our first conversation, she exclaimed, "I remember that phone call like it just happened. I knew you were surviving my worst nightmare. That was reality. Because God was faithful to you, I *knew* he would be faithful to me."

In the months to come Leslie and I shared long conversations and many, many tears as we talked about our boys and our love for them. We imagined them meeting in heaven, watching us, grinning and high fiving each other, exclaiming, "Isn't our God good? Look at our moms. They really want to honor Jesus in this grief work our Father has given them to do. It's so cool that they are friends!"

About a year later Leslie gave me a poem from *Streams in the Desert*. In preparation for writing this book, I asked Leslie to explain how that poem described our friendship. She wrote:

I am convinced that much of what I experienced was *less excruciating* than it might have been for me because of what God took you through first. Because I had you, I knew I was not going through a place no one had been before. Knowing that someone (you) had gotten through this darkness and was still able to glorify our Lord, was, in many ways, what enabled me to keep breathing. Any bit, even a crumb, of what comfort that God supplied for you was magnified in its importance for me.

When I was tempted to stop writing this book, God repeatedly reminded me of Leslie and this poem, which has no attributed author.

If you have gone a little way ahead of me, call back—
T'will cheer my heart and help my feet along the stony
    track;
And if, perchance, Faith's light is dim, because the oil
    is low,
Your call will guide my lagging course as wearily I go.

Call back, and tell me that he went with you into the
    storm;
Call back, and say he kept you when the forest's roots
    were torn;
That, when the heavens thundered and the earthquake
    shook the hill,
He bore you up and held you where the very air was still.

Oh, friend, call back, and tell me for I cannot see your
    face;
They say it glows with triumph, and your feet bound in
    the race;

But there are mists between us and my spirit eyes are
dim,
And I cannot see the glory, though I long for word of
him.

But if you'll say he heard you when your prayer was but
a cry,
And if you'll say he saw you through the night's sin-
darkened sky—
If you have gone a little way ahead, oh, friend, call
back—
T'will cheer my heart and help my feet along the stony
track.[1]

Thinking Biblically, Living Biblically

Why did I say yes to Susan? Because I was a nice person,
kind, loving, longing to help? No. With her, I reluctantly slid
back into the dark abyss of death because of my theology. To survive Mark's death required that I think and act biblically. The
tasks God had given me to do in this journey through grief had
helped solidify my worldview. My desperate search in the weeks
and months right after Mark's death to understand the mysteries
of God forced me to soak in Scripture. And it was there God
reminded me that he created me as part of a family, a community of his children.

Millennia ago he announced to a moon worshiper, Abram,
that he (God) had chosen him (Abram) to be his child. God
renamed Abram as Abraham. God promised Abraham that he
would never again be alone; God would always travel with him.
He also promised that out of Abraham would come a community, a family that would be too big to number, that this family
would experience great blessing and as a result would pass on
those blessings to others. The stunning part about these promises

is that they belong to everyone who trusts Jesus as personal savior (Gal. 2:29). When Susan called, I knew she was asking me to live out my worldview or theology. She expected me to push her request and my feelings through the grid of Scripture. She trusted that because I was committed to thinking biblically, I would respond biblically, no matter what my emotions cried.

As I stood in the back yard and squished my protests through the grid of Scripture, I remembered the promise of God's presence and that as a daughter of the King of kings, I was equipped to extend his compassion to a brokenhearted sister. I had no choice but to pick up the phone and call Leslie. Susan's phone call forced the worldview of my mind to become the worldview of my soul.

THE TREASURE OF THINKING AND ACTING BIBLICALLY

I run in the path of your commands, for you have set my heart free. (Ps. 119:32)

Some people have concluded that to think biblically means to put a straitjacket on our emotions. The straitjacket forces us to bow in submission to God's purposes and stoically live life without ever addressing the gaping wound of shattered dreams. The straitjacket binds us and denies the existence of pain, questions, confusion. For me, thinking biblically frees me to sort out my feelings and determine how I will live each day. Difficult circumstances and family crises have become opportunities for me to intentionally step back and think, "What does God say about this terrible time?" Thinking biblically requires discipline and practice. It becomes the roadmap that directs our steps in this pathway designed for us by God.

The Pathway Marked Out for Me

I made Hebrews 12:1–3 my mantra when the pathway marked out by God for me seemed too hard:

> Therefore, since we are surrounded by such a great cloud of witnesses, let us throw off everything that hinders and the sin that so easily entangles, and let us run with perseverance the race marked out for us. Let us fix our eyes on Jesus, the author and perfector of our faith, who for the joy set before him endured the cross, scorning its shame, and sat down at the right hand of the throne of God. Consider him who endured such opposition from sinful men, so that you will not grow weary and lose heart.

I understood from this Scripture that my life was designed by God and that I had the privilege of living in a way that showed a broken world how he loves his children. I was on my way home, and I had assignments from him that would keep me busy on my journey. God reinforced this message when I read the November 1 entry in *My Utmost for His Highest*:

> There is no such thing as a private life—"a world within the world"—for a man or woman who is brought into fellowship with Jesus Christ's sufferings. God breaks up the private life of his saints, and makes it a thoroughfare for the world on the one hand and for Himself on the other. . . .
>
> If through a broken heart God can bring His purposes to pass in the world, then thank Him for breaking your heart.[2]

From Misery to Mercy to Ministry

It's often in the serving while surrounded by the debris of a broken heart that God brings the very things for which we are praying. It's in serving that we experience God's blessing and strength. When we persevere and keep taking the next step, even when it's painful, God gives us a treasure that produces the energy we need and meets the most private, intimate needs of our souls.

We call this moving from misery to mercy to ministry. Peter challenged the early church to minister to others as evidence that they had experienced God's mercy when they were in misery.

> You are a chosen people, a royal priesthood, a holy nation, a people belonging to God, that you may declare the praises of him who called you out of darkness into his wonderful light. Once you were not a people, but now you are the people of God; once you had not received mercy, but now you have received mercy.
>
> Dear friends, I urge you, as aliens and strangers in the world, to abstain from sinful desires, which war against your soul. Live such good lives among the pagans that, though they accuse you of doing wrong, they may see your good deeds and glorify God on the day he visits us. (1 Peter 2:9–12)

TREASURES OF HOPE

Scriptural Gems

If you are in a wearisome place where you can't imagine helping someone else, don't let these exhortations pile on guilt. Rather, ask God to use the words of Scripture to give you a goal for your journey.

"Praise be to the God and Father of our Lord Jesus Christ, the Father of compassion and the God of all comfort, who comforts us in all our troubles, so that we can comfort those in any trouble with the comfort we ourselves have received from God. For just as the sufferings of Christ flow over into our lives, so also through Christ our comfort overflows." (2 Cor. 1:3–5)

"For we are God's workmanship, created in Christ Jesus to do good works, which God prepared in advance for us to do." (Eph. 2:10)

"Let us consider how we may spur one another on toward love and good deeds. . . . let us encourage one another—and all the more as you see the Day approaching." (Heb. 10:24–25b)

"Preach the Word; be prepared in season and out of season; correct, rebuke and encourage—with great patience and careful instruction." (2 Tim. 4:2)

Songs in the Night: A Mighty Fortress

The words "A mighty fortress is our God" promise strength, courage, and victory in this world where devils threaten to destroy us. Soak in this message based on Psalm 46 as you prayerfully consider how God wants you to call back to those coming behind you in this journey through sorrow.

> A mighty fortress is our God, a bulwark never failing;
> Our helper he amid the flood of mortal ills prevailing.
> For still our ancient foe doth seek to work us woe;
> His craft and pow'r are great; and armed with cruel hate,
> On earth is not his equal.

Did we in our own strength confide, our striving would
     be losing;
Were not the right man on our side, the man of God's
     own choosing.
Dost ask who that may be? Christ Jesus, it is he,
Lord Sabaoth his name, from age to age the same,
And he must win the battle.

And though this world, with devils filled, should
     threaten to undo us,
We will not fear, for God hath willed his truth to tri-
     umph through us.
The prince of darkness grim, we tremble not for him;
His rage we can endure, for lo, his doom is sure;
One little word shall fell him.

That Word above all earthly pow'rs, no thanks to them,
     abideth;
The Spirit and the gifts are ours through him who with
     us sideth.
Let goods and kindred go, this mortal life also;
The body they may kill: God's truth abideth still;
His kingdom is forever.

Other Hopeful Ideas

In the first months of grief, I could not imagine help-ing or comforting anyone. But in the back of my mind, I remembered Scriptures that promised God's enabling power to transform our sorrow into opportunities to com-fort others. A wise friend advised, "Right now your ministry is to let us pray for you and allow your journey to teach us. God will let you know when it's time to help someone else."

Recognize your limitations but don't automatically conclude that you are helpless. Ask a friend to carry the burden with you through specific prayer. Susan's promise to pray for us gave me courage to call Leslie.

A friend's comment that she was learning how to grieve by spending time with me was mystifying. I felt no strength, but her words gave me confidence that God was doing something good. Ask a trusted friend to help you identify some of the treasures God has given you in your journey. Then you will be ready to share them at the appropriate time with someone coming after you in the pathway of grief. As you know, what seems insignificant to one who has never experienced sorrow is a cherished gift to the brokenhearted—for example, the strong voice Leslie heard over the phone.

Jot down the little things people did that comforted you and consider how you can pass on those treasures. A neighbor I barely knew brought over a fresh-baked loaf of zucchini bread two weeks after Mark's death. She shared a story of her daughter's friendship with Mark and left. Food stuck in my throat like dry crumbs those days. She didn't know how much I enjoy toasted and buttered zucchini bread. But God did. Eleven years later I still remember her words and the smell and taste of what she probably thought was an insignificant offering of love.

Author Jo Anne Lyon reminds us that sometimes we make encouragement too complicated:

> The women who stood at the foot of the cross as Jesus was crucified. . . . model for us the power of presence. . . .
> It is not easy to give the gift of presence.
> When presence is not given, both the giver and

receiver lose something. Simple acts of presence such as a phone call, a brief hospital visit, a lingering hello, a warm touch on the arm, or a shared cup of coffee—yes, these are a blessing.[3]

What can you do today that involves the simple "gift of presence"—the gift of being there for someone?

Prayer: Willing to Call Back

Father, at times you seem a hard taskmaster, asking us to use broken hearts to give hope to others. Teach us that obedience to your call is actually a road toward peace and joy. Make us willing to call back to fellow travelers and exclaim, "God is faithful. You can trust him."

15

When You Expect New Mercies . . .

The Treasure of Deeper Understanding

Midnight Principle: If I keep being honest with God, I will eventually understand his love in a deeper way.

Journal Insight

June 19, 1995. You are teaching me a new wonder of your unmerited love as I observe our son with his son. The theology of my mind is becoming the theology of my soul. The night of

Markie's birth, the trauma of our son's death took on new meaning to young Chuck, Markie's daddy. Chuck wept as he held his new little boy in his arms and wondered aloud how his parents (we) had survived the death of our Mark. He wonders at the deep love he has after just a few hours with his child. Suddenly he realizes that as horrific as his grief over losing his brother Mark was, ours as parents is even more horrific. He asked us, "How have you lived with such loss?" He imagines his own feelings if anything were to happen to his new little boy.

New Lessons in Love

Early in my journey a friend encouraged me that if I kept being honest with God, I would one day understand his love in a way I never had before. At the time her words did not compute in my grief-inflamed brain. But the births of our grandchildren gave all of us a new perspective on the treasure of Jesus and the gift of eternal life. I was able to see God's glory in terribly painful moments experienced by our children when their children were born.

A few days before Dan and Laura's daughter, Emma Grace, was born, we gathered as a family to recognize the ninth anniversary of Mark's death. Grandchildren were everywhere, and the adults sat in the sunroom laughing and talking. Suddenly Dan started sobbing. His sobs intensified as he tried to explain. "Mom and Dad, I'm looking at all these grandchildren (six by this time) and the way you love them. I'm thinking about how much I love our little baby already, and I haven't even held her. How have you survived this grief? I can't stand the thought of possibly losing our baby, and she isn't even born. And where is my brother? I want Mark here. He should be here." Laura hugged Dan and wept with him. We knew she was thinking of her mother and asking the same questions.

None of us were surprised by this outburst. Chuck and Heidi told us that minutes after they held their newborn children, they lost control of their emotions and experienced deep grief. We were saddened that such a glorious moment was shadowed by grief. But when you expect God to send you new mercies every day, you start looking for them, especially in the darkness. So even in this anguish was a gift designed by God for me.

New Understanding of Your Redemption Plan

June 19, 1994. Chuck's new awareness of our special parental love and grief for Mark opened my spirit to a deeper understanding of your redemption plan. You created us so that the greatest bond we will have is between a parent and child. Studies show that the greatest wound a human experiences is the trauma of losing a child, and many never recover, are never able to enjoy life again. When Mark and Kelly died, every parent we knew said to us or to others, "I could never survive the loss of my child. Your grief is unthinkable. I can't go there." The terror strikes at the deepest nerve of our being. You tapped into this mysterious bond and wrenching pain.

This is why you chose the sacrifice of your Son as a means to demonstrate your mysterious love to us. In choosing the plan of salvation, you gave your one and only Son!

John 3:16: "For God so loved the world that he gave his one and only Son, that whoever believes in him shall not perish but have eternal life."

Surely the use of these descriptive words is not an accident. You are connecting with the parent-child bond. This is a dimension of your love I have not previously experienced. You acknowledge that what you have done is foolishness to us (1 Cor. 1:18). If I sacrificed my child for others, I would be considered crazy (Rom. 5:7–8). As I consider how I would feel if I had voluntarily given up Mark so his friends would come to you, how angry and unforgiving I would be if they turned their backs on my sacrifice. Why are you so patient?

You cannot tolerate sin. It's only through your one and only Son, Jesus, that I can know your love, that I have experienced your presence. Father, keep opening the eyes of my heart, I want to experience all of your love.

New Understanding of Resting in Our Father's Care

"How great is the love the Father has lavished on us, that we should be called children of God! And that is what we are" (1 John 3:1a).

Before Emma Grace Judith Betters, our seventh grandchild, was born, her dad, Daniel, composed and recorded an acoustical guitar piece he titled "Emma's Song." Pregnant Laura often placed the CD player on her tummy and played this sweet song, even while Daniel in a sing-song voice said, "Your daddy loves you. Your daddy loves you!"

Even before Emma's birth her parents were shaping her worldview. But as a growing infant, she needed more than a song to make her feel safe. When Emma was especially distraught, Laura cupped Emma's cheeks in her long, slender hands. Emma bowed her face into Laura's fingers and pulled the hands even tighter. As the warmth and strength of Mommy's hands flowed into Emma's skin, the sobs subsided and Emma relaxed. Dan expanded her safe zone when he gently taught her that his hands cupping her face could give her the same sense of security, especially at bedtime.

Dan, Laura, and Emma lived with us while their new house was being built. Emma's world now included other people. As she began to trust Grammy and Grandad a little, we encouraged Dan and Laura to go out for an evening. At bedtime, I placed her in the crib and tucked her special blanket around her face, as her daddy had instructed. In the darkness Emma's fat little fingers found my hand and gently pulled it against her cheek. I could feel her body relax and almost sigh in safety.

Emma is learning to trust her parents' care: the warmth of their hands cradling her face, the sound of her daddy singing, "Your daddy loves you. Your daddy loves you," and the background music of the song he wrote for her . . . it doesn't get much better than that. As Emma grows, she will learn that there are times when she will have to obey Mommy and Daddy even when obedience is hard. And there will be more than one time when their response to her "Why?" will be, "Because I said so."

I see how much Daniel and Laura love Emma—I know how much we love our four children—and yet I read Jesus' words, describing his Father in heaven and ours: "Which of you, if his son asks for bread, will give him a stone? Or if he asks for a fish, will give him a snake? If you, then, though you are evil, know how to give good gifts to your children, how much more will your Father in heaven give good gifts to those who ask him!"

(Matt. 7:9–11). I can hardly fathom such a parental love that far outstrips mine or my children's. And in the context of that love for his Son, Jesus, God sent him to redeem his other children. "For God so loved the world that he gave his one and only Son, that whoever believes in him shall not perish but have eternal life" (John 3:16).

Hudson Taylor's words describe his last earthly good-bye to his mother and help us wrap our minds around the deep Fatherlove God has for us:

> My beloved, now sainted mother had come to see me off from Liverpool. Never shall I forget that day, nor how she went with me into the little [ship's] cabin that was to be my home for nearly six long months. With a mother's loving hand she smoothed the little bed. She sat by my side, and joined me in the last hymn that we should sing together before the long parting. We knelt down, and she prayed—the last mother's prayer I was to hear before starting for China. Then notice was given that we must separate, and we had to say good-bye, never expecting to meet on earth again.
>
> For my sake she restrained her feelings as much as possible. We parted; and she went on shore, giving me her blessing! I stood alone on deck, and she followed the ship as we moved toward the dock gates. As we passed through the gates, and the separation really commenced, I shall never forget the cry of anguish wrung from that mother's heart. It went through me like a knife. I never knew so fully, until then, what "God so loved the world" meant. And I am quite sure that my precious mother learned more of the love of God to the perishing in that hour than in all her life before.[1]

THE TREASURE OF DEEPER UNDERSTANDING

Whenever I see Emma's little hands pull her mommy's hands tightly around her face, I think about the author of Psalm 131, who in three short verses describes his transformation from a wailing, exhausted infant who enters this world thinking everything revolves around him into a peaceful, weaned child walking securely at his mother's side. His journey has taught him to quietly wait for his mother to meet his needs.

May 30, 1998. What settled this writer? He concludes that though your ways, Lord, don't make sense, your character makes you trustworthy. You are perfect, therefore you cannot make a mistake. He determines to face life with a full recognition of his own limitations and complete submission to you.

Psalm 131:1: "My heart is not proud, O Lord, my eyes are not haughty; I do not concern myself with great matters or things too wonderful for me."

His words imply that he has struggled to understand the mysteries of disappointment, sorrow, and pain. This writer is a theologian, wrestling to understand your character. I don't sense he gave up on life or that he will stop trying to understand you, but something happened to change his focus from needing to be in control to trusting. His motivation has changed from unraveling the mystery of your mind to resting in your faithful love as a child rests in his mother's care.

He makes a choice: His emotions will not control his actions.

Psalm 131:2: "But I have stilled and quieted my soul; like a weaned child with its mother, like a weaned child is my soul within me."

Grace and choice intertwine. I, too, must make moment-by-moment choices to obey you and accept your purposes for my daily life even when my emotions don't want to submit. . . .

Psalm 131:3: "O Israel, put your hope in the Lord, both now and forevermore."

Trust requires a choice to believe the promise that though you don't remove us from the hard places, you are in them with us. With sweet surrender comes serenity. Perhaps in his pain the writer demanded answers from heaven. But he gave up trying to understand what mortal man cannot understand and encourages his fellow wanderers to do the same.

The theme of redeeming the darkness of the journey by living a life that reflects our hope in you is a strong thread throughout Scripture. It takes every spiritual muscle to step up to such a calling, muscles that require regular exercise. Like the psalmist, I need the mind of a little child to daily face the tasks of each day with purpose and hope, trusting that in your time, you will come for your children. I long for that day.

TREASURES OF HOPE

Scriptural Gems

"I am the good shepherd; I know my sheep and my sheep know me—just as the Father knows me and I know the Father—and I lay down my life for the sheep." (John 10:14–15)

"I pray also for those who will believe in me [Jesus]. . . . I in them and you in me. May they be brought to complete unity to let the world know that you sent me and have loved them even as you have loved me." (John 17:20b, 23)

"This is how God showed his love among us: He sent his one and only Son into the world that we might live through him." (1 John 4:9)

"God is love." (1 John 4:17)

Songs in the Night: He Giveth More Grace

I trust it's been obvious that in the midnight of life God has used old hymns (and also some new ones) to ground me in the truth of his Word, to embrace me in his love, and to strengthen me in my walk. Songs written by people who lived out their faith in physical or emotional pain especially turned my heart toward God. Annie Johnson Flint is one of those credible witnesses whose writings call back to fellow travelers, "God is faithful. God is love. You can trust him!"

Orphaned at a young age, Annie and her sister were adopted by the Flints, a loving, generous couple who taught the girls how to love and honor God. As a young adult Annie lost her adopted parents to death within several months of each other. Facing poverty, Annie turned to a teaching career, but soon severe arthritis left her helpless to care for herself or her fragile sister.

Throughout her long life, Annie refused to whine about her needs and learned deep dependence on God. Her poetry and writings not only expressed her heart but also, through their publication, became a means to pay her bills. When she died in 1919, she could barely hold a pen in her gnarled hands. Every movement was painful. But moments before she moved into the presence of her God, she declared that everything was "all right."

Note especially the last line of the second verse of her powerful song, "He Giveth More Grace": "Our Father's full giving is only begun."

He giveth more grace when the burdens grow greater,
He sendeth more strength when the labors increase;
To added affliction he addeth his mercies.
To multiplied trials his multiplied peace.

When we have exhausted our store of endurance,
When our strength has failed ere the day is half done.
When we reach the end of our hoarded resources
Our Father's full giving is only begun.

His love has no limit, his grace has no measure,
His power no boundaries known unto men;
For out of his infinite riches in Jesus
He giveth and giveth and giveth again.

Other Hopeful Ideas

My friend's cries took me back to the early days of sorrow. She said, "I want to trust God. I've always trusted God. But in response to my longing for intimacy with him, he took my dear, dear husband. I'm bitter. I don't like the way I feel. I can't stay here in this bitterness. But how do I pray for my children and friends to know the love of God when it seems he takes away

what's most precious in order to answer my prayers? His definition of love doesn't fit mine."

This may be your response to a chapter on experiencing the
love of God more deeply in the abyss of grief. It just doesn't compute. There are moments I still struggle to reconcile God's love
with his sovereignty. My dear sister, listen carefully to me. I am
calling back: God is love. When you are his daughter, his arms
hold you tightly in his grip. Your name is written on the palm of
his hand. Slowly force your bruised, spiritual muscles to soak in
the Scriptures above. Write them out in your journal as a prayer
and replace the personal pronouns with your name. Choose to
believe that as you keep on sorting through the shards of your
broken heart, unraveling the tangled balls of sorrow and confusion, that God will answer the cries of your soul. He *will* help
you, even in this.

Prayer: Satisfy That Longing
O Lord, right now one of your brokenhearted children wants
to feel the warmth and strength of a father's hands gently cupping her face, soothing her and whispering, "Your daddy loves
you. Your daddy loves you." Please, Father, satisfy that longing as
only you can.

16

$\mathscr{H}$OW $\mathscr{A}$RE $\mathscr{Y}$OU $\mathscr{T}$RAVELING $\mathscr{H}$EAVENWARD?

THE TREASURE OF HEAVEN

MIDNIGHT PRINCIPLE: There are some wounds that only heaven can heal.

JOURNAL INSIGHT

July 3, 2004. Father, how can I say thanks for the gift you sent our way today? I want a record of it for our children and grandchildren to one day read and exclaim, "Wasn't God good to our mom and dad, our grandparents?" Here's what happened.

Chuck finished cutting the grass and yelled, "Let's get out of here and go somewhere for lunch."

"The traffic will be awful."

"I don't care. I just need to keep moving and get my mind off of this weekend. Bring the flowers for the cross."

I grabbed the bouquet of silk roses, two bottles of water, climbed into the car, and tried not to cry. I thought this year would be easier, eleven years since Mark's homegoing. It should be easier. Instead, both of us were weary from fighting tears and trying to stay busy. We inched along the same highway Mark traveled that fateful night. Thousands of people appeared to have the same itch to get out of their houses. A trip that should have taken a half hour took three times as long.

We parked the car and walked to a restaurant we'd never patronized. At our request, the hostess seated us at an outside table where we could watch the herons soar over the water. Rock music played softly in the background. After ordering, Chuck and I sat in silence, not looking at each other for fear of unleashing tears.

Suddenly our ears perked up. Both of us recognized the music that now loudly played, a completely different genre than the past fifteen minutes. We looked around to see if anyone else noticed. Everyone seemed oblivious to the words of the popular Christian song playing on the secular rock station. "I can only imagine what it will be like. . . ."[1]

Chuck covered my hand with his, and held-back tears started dropping. Though familiar with the words, we listened carefully, sensing this was a message from you, Lord, reminding us that Mark is experiencing things beyond our wildest imaginations, encouraging us to remember we are one day closer to seeing you, when our imagining will become reality. Heaven, our real home.

At the end of the song, the volume of the rock music dropped back to its original level, leaving us with the conclusion that this was a treasure in the darkness, letting us know that eleven years later you had not forgotten us.

Heaven, My Real Home

A book on the treasures God gives in the dark night of the soul would not be complete without a chapter on the hope of heaven. Chuck often says that Mark's death unbolted us from our love affair with this world. Leslie Singenstreu says that when Susan repeated that statement to her after Zach's death, she could hear the chains falling on the floor around her.

In the months after losing Mark, I was convinced that the only thing that would heal me would be for Jesus to come and take us all home. I had fleeting moments of wanting to die myself. It seemed easier to physically die than to die to self and live on this earth for God's glory. One evening I heard our son, Daniel, on the phone, sobbing to a friend, "Jesus needs to come back now. There is no other way this pain will go away. We need heaven, right now." His friend was unable to comfort him, and Dan's sobs grew louder. I told him to hang up the phone and come into our bedroom. He threw his manly six-foot-frame across the foot of the bed. I held his head in my lap and wiped the tears from his cheeks.

That evening, we encouraged Dan to thank God for the many good times he had shared with Mark even though remembering was painful. We talked a lot about the growing up years and the way they always shared life. We often joked that to make life exciting Mark depended on Dan as his social director. Dan and his friends saw younger Mark as a peer and included him in adventures, such as volleyball and surfing trips, that most boys his age would not have enjoyed. The problem with these memories, though, was that Dan wanted more. He wanted to know his brother as a grown man, not frozen as a teenager. When he went to bed, Chuck and I struggled to find the right comfort; we came up empty.

What's It Like?

My youngest child was in heaven, and my pathway on earth would one day lead me to the same destination. I wanted to know everything I could about this mysterious, wonderful, perfect, tear-free place. I cross-referenced every Scripture that slightly alluded to eternity. I soaked up books and sermons on heaven.

I spent hours walking and listening to Joni Eareckson Tada's audio book, *Heaven: Your Real Home*. Passersby probably wondered at this strange woman who walked miles with tears streaming down her cheeks. I reveled with Joni over her imaginations of what heaven will be like and wondered if she had read my journal, because our conclusions were so similar. I laughed out loud with expectation of my first moments in the presence of my Savior, and I wondered who would greet me at the gate. I sometimes think about all those who have traveled this pathway ahead of me and are already home. Are they gleefully helping prepare the places for their spiritual brothers and sisters? Are they antici-pating with wonder and joy our arrival? Does the word go out in heaven when one of their spiritual family members is on their way? Would Mark greet me with his smile and gloriously blue eyes and exclaim, "See, Mom? It's all true! It's all true!" Of course, I have no scriptural answers, but God's Word seems to encourage my imaginings (1 Cor. 2:9).

The Truck Driver with a Message

There is danger in longing to know about things that God doesn't explain, and there is a tendency in our world to proclaim as truth those things that are not. We tested every glimmer of heaven by the grid of God's Word. We placed no hope in anything that was not his truth. But our emotional and spiritual senses were on full alert as we slogged through the pathway of grief. Young Chuck had a particularly interesting conversation with a stranger that puzzles us to this day.

Early in 1993, before Mark died, Chuck first heard and then saw a stranger in the church building, before services on a Sunday morning. He heard a man wailing. Following the sound, he found a middle-aged, balding man prostrated on a classroom floor. He was crying out in prayer, not for himself but for our community, for the children of the world, for the wayward teenagers, for people to repent. Chuck left him alone and went back to the sanctuary to practice his piano playing. But soon the man came and talked to him.

Chuck explains, "I had never met a man like this before. His face was red and swollen from crying, yet he was a burly fellow—a man's man—not someone you would mess with. He had a maturity about him, not unstable as you might infer from his great display of emotion."

He said he was a truck driver who just happened to stop at the church to pray. They talked about the church and about his burden for people to turn to Jesus. He left before the service.

But after that, every month or so, he showed up again, crying out in prayer in a classroom. If Chuck was in the building, the trucker would talk with him, offer encouragement or prayer, and then leave. Chuck says, "I remember thinking that this guy was different—nothing bad—just something different."

Then Mark was killed, in July. And in September Chuck began having the dreams I mentioned in chapter 7. The morning after he'd heard the otherworldly music, he went to the church. And guess who was there? The praying, crying truck driver. Chuck explains, "He hadn't been by for a while. I really didn't feel like talking to him. I thought I'd slip into the church office and avoid him. Sure enough he found me. I said, 'hi,' then turned to some task, trying to make it obvious that today wasn't a good time to shoot the breeze. He talked to our secretaries, but after a while I could feel his gaze on me—almost looking through me. I turned toward him and saw his eyes; they looked like blue lightning. When he spoke to me, the room froze. The other people in the room didn't hear him speak; only I did. 'Do you know what heaven's like, Chuck? I'll tell you about heaven because I've seen it. There are great reunions of loved ones every day. It is real—don't worry about anything—it's real, and you'll see your brother again.' "

That was the last time Chuck saw the truck driver, which he—and we—believe was no ordinary trucker but an angel (Heb. 13:2) sent to remind us of the heavenly home that awaits us.

Chuck says, "God promises to raise my dead body when Jesus comes back. Why would I think it's too hard for him to send an angel disguised as a truck driver to turn my heart toward his truth? I think he condescends sometimes to meet us right where we are, never at the expense of his Word and never by adding to his Word (Joel 2:28). Our family needed revival. We needed God to pour his Spirit all over us. This was one of those moments where he gave me hope that he was doing just that, in his way, his time."

A Changing Desire

God tells us just enough about heaven to whet our appetite and make us long for more when, through Paul, he declares, "No eye has seen, no ear has heard, no mind has conceived what God has prepared for those who love him" (1 Cor. 2:9).

The more I learned about heaven, the more real my destination became. Slowly my longing for heaven transitioned from longing for Mark to an intense desire to be with my Savior and my God. On the anniversaries of the deaths of Mark and his friend Kelly, we exchange cards with Kelly's family. The first year, Kelly's sister wrote, "We are one year closer." We knew she meant that we were one year closer to heaven, our real home, the place where tears have no purpose and will be wiped away (Rev. 21:4).

Out of the Mouths of Babes

Because our family regularly talks about heaven as a real place, it's no surprise that the children in our family think of it as a desired destination, A few years ago, Danielle, our daughter's child, made it clear that she's ready to go—when Mommy and Daddy are ready! Five-year-old Markie, however, was ready for adventure, and if heaven was such a great place, why wait?

Our grandson rushed into the sunroom with his usual enthusiasm. Markie anticipated a fun day with Grammy but needed to settle some deep issues first. "Grammy!" my grandson exclaimed. "I want to go to heaven today!"

His parents had already warned us that Markie regularly expressed his desire for heaven. Although he has never met his

Uncle Mark or Grandmom Judy (his mother's mother), they were real to him because we talked about them as part of our family. He had prayed for Mr. Dave and Aunt Fran and he understood that though God had not healed them on this earth, they were now with Jesus. Why wouldn't everyone want to go to heaven if they could?

I prayed silently for wisdom.

"Markie, this is a good day to go to heaven! I want to go, too!" I laughed.

Markie's eyes lit up. Finally, an ally!

"Then let's go!" he shouted.

"Well, Markie, there's a problem. Only Jesus can decide when it's time for us to go to heaven."

"But why can't Jesus say that this is the day?"

"Markie, we don't get to go to heaven until our work on earth is done. And only Jesus knows when that is." I wondered if he could understand something that most adults can't.

He stared at me as he processed this amazing thought. Finally, he had hope that there was a way to get to heaven quickly. He slowly looked around the room at the piles of packages and wrapping paper and then exclaimed, "Grammy, let's hurry up and wrap those packages so that we can finish our work and then we can go to heaven today!"

I grabbed my sweet grandson, hugged him tightly, and laughed, "Markie, this is only one job. Jesus might have lots more for us to do, and we have to trust him to decide when we're finished. In the meantime, we need to keep obeying and loving him."

Later his parents told us that every time Markie saw someone working, he would rush over, pick up a hammer, and beg, "Let me help you get your work finished because as soon as all the work is done, we get to go to heaven!"

The First Thing I Want to Do

A few months after Markie proclaimed his longing for heaven, his mother, Melanie, told me this story. "Mom, this morning I was teaching Markie that the first thing we get to do when go to heaven is throw our crowns at the feet of Jesus. I explained to him that our crowns are our reward for our obedience, for the work that we do here on earth. For a few seconds he seriously considered my words and then asked, 'Mommy, is that the first thing we have to do when we get to heaven?'

"I wanted to impress on him the privilege we have to honor Christ in this way, so I said, 'Markie, that's the first thing we *get* to do.'

" 'But, Mommy, the first thing I want to do when I get to heaven is hug Jesus, and then I'll throw my crowns at his feet.' "

Me too, Markie! Me, too.

The Treasure of Heaven

We have this hope as an anchor for the soul, firm and secure. It enters the inner sanctuary behind the curtain, where Jesus, who went before us, has entered on our behalf. (Heb. 6:19–20)

A ship's anchor keeps it safe when it rests deep in the earth below the water. Our hope in Christ is a guarantee of our safe passage from this earth to heaven and moors us to God. With unflinching hope, we look forward to the day our imaginings of heaven become reality.

Our research for writing *Treasures of Faith* gave me deep insight into living life today in the context of the hope of heaven. The people described in Hebrews 11 demonstrate that the pathway of faith is filled with potholes and unexpected twists and turns. Applauded by God for trusting him, they know nothing of the prosperity gospel touted by "health and wealth" preachers. They would agree with the friend who wrote in a sympathy note, "There are some wounds that only heaven can heal." When I read that many of these people died without seeing the promises fulfilled but died trusting God, I began to relax in God's unfailing love:

> All these people were still living by faith when they died. They did not receive the things promised; they only saw them and welcomed them from a distance. And they admitted that they were aliens and strangers on earth. People who say such things show that they are looking for a country of their own. If they had been thinking of the country they had left, they would have had opportunity to return. Instead, they were longing for a better country—a heavenly one. Therefore God is not ashamed to be called their God, for he has prepared a city for them. (Heb. 11:13–16)

The pressure for him to take care of me my way this minute was suddenly gone. I understood that there *are* some wounds that only heaven can heal. In heaven there will be no more tears, crying, or death (Rev. 21:3–4). But until then, God will walk with me in the valley of tears, and I can wait for him to keep his promises in his timing, even if that means waiting until I arrive in heaven.

Even as I write these words, I can barely see the page because of the anticipation of the treasures God has planned for his children!

Sometimes God brings people across my path who are not only suffering great loss but also have no assurance that their loved one is in heaven. I recognized the hollow look of the woman standing in line to speak to me and braced myself for her question. "Mark's declaration of his faith in Christ gives you such comfort. But when I'm all alone and really honest about the faith of my son, I'm not confident that I will see him in heaven. I'm not sure he loved Jesus. How can God comfort me in my grief?"

I hugged her tightly and sighed deeply. This brokenhearted mother had just heard me speak about the glory of heaven and my confidence that because of Mark's trust in Jesus, I would see him again. What words could answer her question? Only the God of all comfort (2 Cor. 1:3–4) can satisfy such an anguished cry.

I had only a few minutes before my next message so I quickly prayed that God would give this woman hope through my response. "You are a woman of integrity, because you are honestly confronting all the questions of your grief. No one but God knows the human heart. He is perfect mercy and justice. When you are wracked with fear for your son's eternal life, God is asking you to trust that your child is in his merciful and just hands. The story of the thief on the cross who trusted Jesus just before his death reminds us that salvation is all about what Jesus does for us; it's not about our good works. That story is one more reflection of God's great mercy. It comforts us to know that even in the last seconds of physical life, God's children can respond to him."

When I get to heaven, I hope to spend lots of time with a woman I have not physically met but whose life has encouraged me to always look to Jesus. I learned about this godly woman in her book titled *Heaven Opened: The Correspondence of Mary Winslow.* Her son Octavius compiled her writings in a way that touched my soul and turned my heart toward God. Her life story as summarized in the foreword of the book captured my attention. I sensed she and her writings were a credible witness to the faithfulness of God.

Shortly after immigrating to New York with ten children, Mary Winslow lost her infant daughter. Before the baby could be buried, she received word from overseas that her husband had died. Widowed at forty, responsible for nine children, and scarcely settled in America, she was overwhelmed for some months by spiritual darkness and despondency. But in time the Lord turned her darkness into light. Later, she realized that the affliction had been for her welfare. "I think I have learned more of my dreadfully wicked heart, and the preciousness of Jesus during this trial than I ever learnt before." By seasoned experience, she learned how to maintain a spirit of unwavering faith during suffering.[2] Mary used letter writing as a means to encourage others to stay focused on their journey toward heaven. In a letter titled "Looking to Jesus" she exhorted a friend:

> I feel it a pressing duty constantly to encourage, admonish, and exhort those who are walking in the narrow path to hold fast their confidence, and keep *looking to Jesus*. . . . When we see Jesus at the right hand of God waiting to receive us home—when we realize that a very few steps we have to take and then we shall have done with time, and a vast eternity burst upon us with all its solemn and glorious realities, oh, how does the world, with all its tinsel and toys, its emptiness and nothingness, sink into the dust beneath our feet![3]

But the most profound challenge from her writings that has stayed with me is a question she addresses to a new widow: "How are you traveling heavenward?" It is the question I now set before myself every day, as I await my own welcome into the presence of my sovereign Lord, my loving Father, my redeeming Savior. And there to welcome me, I know I will see my smiling son.

Treasures of Hope

Scriptural Gems

"Do not let your hearts be troubled. Trust in God; trust also in me. In my Father's house are many rooms; if it were not so, I would have told you. I am going there to prepare a place for you. And if I go and prepare a place for you, I will come back and take you to be with me that you also may be where I am. You know the way to the place where I am going." (John 14:1–4)

"And I heard a loud voice from the throne saying, 'Now the dwelling of God is with men, and he will live with them. They will be his people, and God himself will be with them and be their God. He will wipe every tear from their eyes. There will be no more death or mourning or crying or pain, for the old order of things has passed away.'

He who was seated on the throne said, 'I am making everything new!' Then he said, 'Write this down, for these words are trustworthy and true.' " (Rev. 21:3–5)

"Listen, I tell you a mystery: We will not all sleep, but we will all be changed—in a flash, in the twinkling of an eye, at the last trumpet. For the trumpet will sound, the dead will be raised imperishable, and we will be changed." (1 Cor. 15:51–52)

Songs in the Night: Great Is Thy Faithfulness

"I remember my affliction and my wandering, the bitterness and the gall. I well remember them, and my soul is downcast within me. Yet this I call to mind and therefore I have hope: Because of the Lord's great love we are not consumed, for his compassions never fail. They are new every morning; great is your faithfulness. I say to myself, 'The Lord is my portion; therefore I will wait for him.' . . . Though he brings grief, he will show compassion, so great is his unfailing love" (Lam. 3:19–24, 32).

On July 6, 1993, I begged God to give me back my child. When he refused, I pleaded for a recipe, a timeline that clarified when my heart would stop aching. The anguish drove me back to the foundations of my faith where I unpacked each belief and examined it through the grid of his Word. Rather than a recipe for grief relief, I found the promise of an eternal intimate relationship. I looked for God everywhere. Nothing was insignificant. It still isn't.

Just as life didn't begin when Mark was born, life didn't stop because Mark died—as much as I thought it should. God increased our family with marriages and grandchildren. We faced deaths as well. Five years after the loss of Mark my mother died.

Before her death, she asked that we sing "Great is Thy Faithfulness" at her memorial service. The familiar tune carried me back to childhood memories of lustily singing this hymn as well as a moving conversation my sister Bonnie had with my mother after our son Chuck had performed with a symphony orchestra. Bonnie exclaimed, "Mommy, you and daddy must be so proud tonight! Not just because of Chuck's accomplishments but because all of your children and grandchildren love Jesus and serve him." Bonnie rushed to her side when she started crying and asked, "Mommy, what is it? Did I say something wrong?" Our mother spoke quietly. "It's grace. It's all of grace. Your father and I can't take credit for any of this. We did so many things wrong. I don't know why God has blessed our family this way. It's grace. All of grace."

The writer of "Great Is Thy Faithfulness" probably whispered the same words about his life.

Insurance Agent Thomas O. Chisolm certainly had his share of disappointments in life. His health had been fragile, forcing him to resign as a Methodist minister after only one year of service. But he enjoyed writing and submitted his poetry to various Christian magazines. Sometimes he got rejection slips, sometimes acceptances, but he seldom received any money. He earned his meager living selling life insurance.

When he was seventy-five, he wrote, "My income has not been large at any time due to impaired health in the earlier years which has followed me on until now. Although I must not fail to record here the unfailing faithfulness of a covenant-keeping God and that He has given me many wonderful displays of His providing care, for which I am filled with astonishing gratefulness."[4]

> Great is Thy faithfulness, O God my Father,
> There is no shadow of turning with Thee;
> Thou changest not, Thy compassions they fail not;
> As Thou hast been Thou forever wilt be.
>
> [Refrain]
> Great is Thy faithfulness!
> Great is Thy faithfulness!
> Morning by morning new mercies I see;
> All I have needed Thy hand hath provided –
> Great is Thy faithfulness, Lord unto me!
>
> Summer and winter, and springtime and harvest,
> Sun, moon and starts in their courses above
> Join with all nature in manifold witness
> To Thy great faithfulness, mercy and love.
>
> Pardon for sin and a peace that endureth,
> Thine own dear presence to cheer and to guide;
> Strength for today and bright hope for tomorrow,
> Blessings all mine, with ten thousand beside!

Like my mother, I have to exclaim, "I've done so much wrong in this journey through grief, yet God has not forsaken me." "Morning by morning new mercies I see." It's grace, it's all of grace.

The night of my mother's death I imagined Mark greeting her in heaven, grinning and exclaiming, "Grandmother, what took you so long! Wait until you see what God has prepared for you!"

And now I imagine that some day, when God takes me from this earth to be in his presence, I will join untold numbers of his children. But I won't feel lost in the crowd, I will feel at home as I never have before. We will experience grace in a way we can't on this earth. We'll catch one another's eye and nod, acknowledging that yes, it's true! Everything we have hoped for and believed—it's true. After Jesus' embrace, I imagine Mark leading the welcoming committee, shouting, "Mom, what took you so long! Wait until you see what God has prepared for you!"

I can only imagine.

Other Hopeful Ideas

"Lord, how am I traveling heavenward?" That's the question I suggest you answer in your journal. Review some of the Scriptures and principles of this book and record which one has had the greatest impact on you. List and describe the practical ways you will apply that truth to your journey heavenward.

Perhaps a better question for some readers is "*Are* you traveling heavenward?" If you're not sure, reread chapter 15. It's my prayer that God will give you clear demonstration that God is faithful in the midnights of the lives of his children. Be sure that you have been justified by faith, so that you are an heir of God, having the hope of eternal life.

If you are having trouble focusing on the hope of heaven, read *Heaven: Your Real Home* by Joni Eareckson Tada. If reading is too difficult, listen to audiotapes of this book.

Prayer: Heavenly Minded

O Father, teach us how to be so heavenly minded that we are earthly good . . . that the thought of heaven will make us more intentional about our pathway here on earth.

Sharon W. Betters is the author of *Treasures of Encouragement* and the *Treasures of Encouragement* daily planner. She also co-authored *Treasures of Faith* with her husband, Chuck Betters. She has written freelance articles for such publications as *Today's Christian Woman, Virtue, Christian Parenting Today,* and *The PCA Messenger.*

She ministers to other women through speaking, writing, counseling, and encouraging. Having experienced the encouragement of the Savior and his people through the heart-wrenching loss of her son, Mark, Sharon is able to communicate with authenticity that same encouragement to others.

Sharon has been a women's Bible study teacher and pastor's wife since 1969, including her current service at Glasgow Reformed Presbyterian Church in Delaware. She is also Executive Director of MARK INC Ministries.

She is also a breast cancer survivor. Her article "My Battle with Breast Cancer," which appeared in *Today's Christian Woman*, has been reprinted in *Amazing Love* (Tyndale House), a compilation of personal women's stories.

Sharon lives in Bear, Delaware with her husband, Chuck, and near her children. She has ten grandchildren.

NOTES

Introduction

1. Brenda Waggoner, *The Velveteen Woman* (Colorado Springs: Chariot Victor, 2002), 187–88.

Chapter 2: Things That Go Bump in the Dark

1. Rose Marie Miller, *From Fear to Freedom: Living as Sons and Daughters of God* (Wheaton, Ill.: Harold Shaw, 1994), 30.

2. This hymn was written by a Plymouth Brethren devotional speaker, Samuel Trevor Francis (1834–1925). Francis wrote it for singing without instruments in unstructured home meetings. Bobbie Wolgemuth writes in *O Worship the King*, "The purpose of the hymn singing was to give the worshipers a clear picture of their position in Christ—His love, His salvation, and their need for holiness and obedience. The original text to 'O the Deep, Deep Love of Jesus' gave a beautiful word picture of the all-encompassing love of the Savior. The rolling tones of the minor key to which it was set provided an introspective and unforgettable experience of worship." Joni Eareckson Tada, John MacArthur, Robert and Bobbie Wolgemuth, *O Worship the King* (Wheaton, Ill.: Crossway, 2000), 34.

Chapter 3: Memorial Stones

1. D. A. Carson, *New Bible Commentary, 21st-Century Edition* (Downers Grove, Ill.: InterVarsity Press, 1994), 580.

2. For more on this incredible story of God's faithfulness and the crossover principle, see Chuck and Sharon Betters, *Treasures of Faith* (Phillipsburg, N.J.: P&R, 1999), chap. 9.

3. If *Ebenezer* is just too old-fashioned a word for you, you might resonate with this adaptation from *The Hymnal 1982* (Episcopal), which includes a favorite word of mine: "Here I find my greatest treasure; hither by thy help I'm come."

4. 1 Chronicles 16:12: "Remember the wonders he has done, his miracles, and the judgments he pronounced."

5. Job 36:24: "Remember to extol his work, which men have praised in song."

Chapter 4: The Darkest Midnight

1. *Washington Post Magazine*, June 13, 1982, 10.

Chapter 5: Leaning into the Pain

1. Cathy McBride, "Blessed Are Those Who Weep," *Today's Christian Woman*, July–August 1987, 39.

2. Ingrid Trobisch, *Keeper of the Springs* (Sisters, Ore.: Multnomah, 1997), 67–68.

3. As quoted in William F. Rogers, *Ye Shall Be Comforted* (Philadelphia: Westminster Press, 1950), 80.

Chapter 6: Wrestling to Rest

1. Marilyn Willett Heavilin, *Roses in December, Finding Strength within Grief* (Eugene: Ore.: Harvest House, 1987).

2. God to Abram (Gen. 15:1); Isaac (Gen. 26:24); Moses (Ex. 3:12); Moses to Joshua (Deut. 30:8); God to Joshua (Josh. 1:5); angel to Gideon (Judg. 6:12); God to Gideon (Judg. 6:16); God to Jeremiah (Jer. 1:8); Jesus to us (Matt. 28:18–20); God to us (Heb. 13:5).

3. David Biebel, *If God Is So Good, Why Do I Hurt So Bad?* (Grand Rapids, Mich.: Revell, 2000), 34.

4. Ibid., 37.

Chapter 7: Echoes of Mercy

1. *When God Doesn't Make Sense* (September 1993, Dr. Chuck Betters. For information on ordering CD or audio cassettes of Chuck's messages, contact MARK INC Ministries, 2880 Summit Bridge Road, Bear, DE 190701, 1-877-MARKINC or visit the web site at www.MARKINC.org.

Chapter 8: Who's Bearing Whose Burden?

1. Northeast Regional Conference, Hershey Hotel, October 1993. Citing Oswald Chambers, *My Utmost for His Highest*, entry for November 1.

2. Sharon W. Betters, *Treasures of Encouragement: Women Helping Women in the Church* (Phillipsburg, N.J.: P&R, 1996).

3. Ibid., 72.

4. For practical ideas on how to encourage someone in deep pain, see *Treasures of Encouragement*.

Chapter 9: Even in Exile, Choosing Life

1. Graham Kendrick, "Shine, Jesus, Shine" (Makeway Music, 1987).

Chapter 11: Safely Gathered In

1. Oswald Chambers, *My Utmost for His Highest* (Westwood, N.J.: Barbour and Company, 1963), entry for April 26.

2. Bodie Thoene, *In My Father's House* (Minneapolis: Bethany, 1992), 278–79.

Chapter 12: It's Not about Me

1. Carolina Sandell Berg, translated by Andrew L. Skoog. Berg wrote more than 650 hymns, which fueled Pietest revivals in Sweden in the late nineteenth century.

Chapter 13: Permission to Enjoy

1. Evelyn Bence, *Prayers for Girlfriends and Sisters and Me* (Ann Arbor, Mich.: Servant, 1990), 28.

Chapter 14: Call Back

1. Author unknown, *Streams in the Desert*, compiled by Mrs. Charles E. Cowman (Grand Rapids: Zondervan, 1965), entry for December 19.

2. Oswald Chambers, *My Utmost for His Highest* (New York: Dodd, Mead: 1935), entry for November 1.

3. Jo Anne Lyon, *The Ultimate Blessing* (Indianapolis: Wesleyan Publishing House, 2003), 42–43.

Chapter 15: When You Expect New Mercies . . .

1. J. Hudson Taylor, *A Retrospect* (Philadelphia: The China Inland Mission, n.d.), 39–40.

Chapter 16: How Are You Traveling Heavenward?

1. Bart Millard, "I Can Only Imagine" (Simpleville Music, 1995).

2. Octavius Winslow, *Heaven Opened: The Correspondence of Mary Winslow* (Grand Rapids: Reformation Heritage Books, 2001), foreword.

3. Ibid., 121–22.

4. From *The One Year Book of Hymns: 365 Devotional Readings Based on Great Hymns of the Faith.* Compiled and edited by Robert K. Brown and Mark R. Norton. Devotions written by William J. Petersen and Randy Petersen (Wheaton, Ill.: Tyndale, 1995), entry for October 15.

Treasures of Encouragement
Women Helping Women in the Church

Women will find both deep comfort and encouragement in this book. Betters explains how the freedom that springs from a secure identity in Christ enables women to reach out to others.

"As women study and implement the deep truths in this book, the body of Christ will be strengthened and blessed."
— SUSAN HUNT

0-87552-097-9, 215 pages, $10.99

Treasures of Encouragement
A Monthly Planner

This beautifully illustrated planner can be started at any time, combining stories and key principles from the book with months-at-a-glance, devotional thoughts, and encouragement ideas.

0-87552-172-X, 80 pages, $14.99

Treasures of Faith
Living Boldly in View of God's Promises

Where others see only suffering, faith enables us to see God's hand drawing us to Himself.

"Chuck and Sharon Betters know the comfort and power of God's embrace in tragedy . . . Here is faith as realistic as the messy challenges of life, and as precious as the mystery of the unlimited love of the Savior."
— BRYAN CHAPELL

0-87552-096-0, 270 pages, $12.99

Treasures of Faith Leader's Guide

Share the treasures of this book with those around you! This thirteen-lesson supplement is ideal for small group settings.

0-87552-094-04, 76 pages, $11.99

P U B L I S H I N G

1-800-631-0094 ✦ WWW.PRPBOOKS.COM